CASE CRITICAL

CASE CRITICAL

THE DILEMMA OF SOCIAL WORK IN CANADA

BEN CARNIOL

between the lines

Published by
Between The Lines
229 College Street,
Toronto, Ontario
Canada M5T 1R4

Cover design by Noel Thomas
Typeset by Coach House Press
Printed in Canada

Between The Lines receives financial assistance from
the Canada Council and the Ontario Arts Council.

Canadian Cataloguing in Publication Data

Carniol, Ben
    Case Critical

Bibliography: p. 000
ISBN 0-919946-80-1 (bound)
ISBN 0-919946-77-1 (pbk.)

1. Social service – Canada.   2. Social workers – Canada.
I. Title.

HV105.C67 1987   361'.971 C87-093493-7

Contents

Preface

SOME SIX YEARS AGO Between the Lines encouraged me to begin writing about the realities of social work and its caseloads, something that would capture the experiences of both those who receive and those who deliver social services. It had been my observation that much of the writing in social work was remote from the realities. In fact, social work students often complain that the theories they learn have little connection with their future work. Although social work textbooks are concerned about social conditions, they seem to evade the critical questions. Does the present system promote personal and community well-being? Or does it serve other priorities? Is social work being used in ways that contradict its official intentions?

To address these questions I have built upon the critical analysis developed by others, supplemented by my own experiences and interviews with social work providers and consumers. My experiences are located in Montreal in the late 1960s and early 1970s, in Calgary until the early 1980s, and most recently in Toronto; the interviews took place in Halifax, Toronto, Calgary, and Vancouver over the past five years, with the most recent ones confirming the earlier findings.

Fortunately, the whole task was shared by many other people who played key roles in helping me bring the work to completion. Robert Clarke of Between The Lines patiently provided guidance and encouragement throughout the long period of writing. With a sharp eye for the political implications of the evidence I was gathering, Robert helped me to become more explicit in perspective.

Although earlier drafts contained insights from feminist analysis, it was Helen Levine who provided thorough and detailed feedback in this area and who thereby helped to place the role of women and women's conditions and struggles at centre stage. I am grateful for the time, skill, and care that went into her numerous excellent suggestions, most of which became integrated within the following pages.

Frieda Forman of the Women's Educational Resource Centre was immensely generous in sharing her time and expertise and helped me track down a wide range of materials on gender relations.

During the early stages of the book's preparation Jamie Swift met with me a number of times, drawing from his own experiences as author and political activist to provide useful advice that helped to give shape to the book.

David Woodsworth (McGill University), Pat Kerans (Dalhousie University), and Elaine Phillips, a social worker in Winnipeg, provided useful and extensive critical comments on earlier drafts. Sheila Neysmith and Victor Marshall (both from the University of Toronto) gave helpful advice on individual chapters in earlier drafts. Michael Lyons of the Labour Council of Metro Toronto facilitated my learning about the issues, priorities, and current projects within the labour movement. Mary Hegan from the Canadian Association of Social Workers and David Thornley from the Social Planning Council of Metro Toronto helped me to obtain updated information and statistics.

When the work was near completion, Anne Swarbrick of the Labour Council of Metro Toronto, Ernie Lightman of the University of Toronto's Faculty of Social Work, and Shalom Schachter from the Ontario Nurses Association read specific sections and helped to improve the text. John MacDonald, social policy analyst and activist from London-Edinburgh and Lancashire, gave freely of his time to review the book, and inspired its title. Ann Phelps of Fax not only input a very messy manuscript but also made useful suggestions for improving it, especially in word usage. Marg Anne Morrison of Between The Lines and Kate Hamilton of Fax and Coach House Press saw the book through production.

To the following Deans and Directors in social work education: Marvyn Novick for affirming the urgency of my completing this book; Carol Baines and Sheila Joel for providing me with a supportive work environment; Tim Tyler for encouraging me to begin; and Len Richards for allowing me the time to proceed.

Special thanks go to the women and men and, in some cases, children, who agreed to be interviewed and who took considerable risks in being candid and in sharing painful realities. I am also grateful to the social workers who shed light on their work environment and on the pressures of their jobs. In most cases their names remain anonymous to protect their positions. Excerpts from these interviews occur throughout the book, usually offset and in italics.

Others across the country helped me to obtain access to interviews and other information. They include: Patsy George, Roop Seebaran, Esther Rausenberg, Marjorie Martin, Penny Stewart, Gordon Hauka, Jack MacDonald, Gus Long, Tom Baker, Carolyn Anderson, Peggy Mayes, Susan Skerry, Heather Lockert, Emily Drzymala, David Baxter, Nelson Gutnick, Joan Ryan, Jim Allison, Maureen Wilson, Dennis Switzer, Elwood Springman, Harvey Stalwick, Graham Riches, Brad McKenzie, Jim Carter, Jim Chang, Mike Keyes, Anne Parsons, Dorothy Moore, Jim Albert, Doris Marshall, Dena and Stan Sugarbroad, Bill Lee, Jenny Green, Gordon Morwood, Mary Kozak, Michael Posluns, Brigitte Kitchen, Janet Mays, Gail Aitken, and Lorna Hurl.

This preface would remain incomplete if I did not express my appreciation to those who were closest to me while working on this project: my family. Rhona's affection kept my motivation high; Mira's sensitivity often taught me more than I could teach her; and Naomi's smile reminded me of why social change is urgent. To my mother and larger extended family goes my acknowledgement of their influence in teaching me not only to listen but also to hear and care about the well-being of others.

This book is dedicated to everyone who helped me in various ways to complete this work, and to the women and men who commit their work, play, and struggle to the construction of a caring and authentically democratic society.

B.C., February 1987

1

Social Work and The Public Conscience

If you really love us, how come you can't do nothin' about our conditions?

a teenage client

I've gone out on calls in the middle of the night. I wasn't on duty at the time but when you get a phone call like that from a family in crisis you go and do what you can. It's as if social workers have become the conscience for the public so that the public can forget about these problems.

a social worker

SOCIAL WORKERS – like their clients – are under pressure. At times they feel beset from all sides: from dissatisfied clients, from their managers, from official policy, from politicians pushing cutbacks in social services, from a sense of failure at having daily to confront a bottomless pit of social problems. Yet their job is to provide help – "social security" – to people in need, the "clients".

As for the clients, evidence shows that they often find themselves blamed for their own problems. They find they don't get the help they need or they don't get nearly enough help to make a difference

5

– or they get "cut off". Yet they are told in turn that this country has a solid package of social programs, at their service.

In the wider community there is an expectation that with all the money being spent on social programs there will at least be a reduction of social problems. Yet the public suspects that the problems are not being reduced. On the contrary, they seem to be worsening. Not surprisingly, the public is highly ambivalent towards social work. There might be praise, for example, when a social worker protects children from violent abuse. But when it comes to trying to ensure that the poor get financial aid, social workers are sometimes seen as bleeding hearts using up taxpayers' money to help lazy bums get something for nothing.

Part of the problem is that social workers and social welfare institutions are functioning in ways that are very different from the ways described and publicized by the profession itself. In truth, because of the constant push of pressures and contradictions, social work in practice takes on a different hue than the picture that, for example, social work textbooks paint for eager students about to enter the profession.

Social work claims to offer effective help to the troubled and the needy. It is one of society's answers to the problems of poverty and social distress. It is aimed at the satisfaction and protection of basic human rights and needs: from living unmolested to having enough money available for housing, food, and clothing. Yet poverty persists, unabated. People freeze to death on the winter streets of our cities for lack of a decent and stable place to stay. Studies show that the gap between rich and poor continues to increase, that wealth continues to concentrate.[1] So too, women are still economically behind men, just as non-whites still suffer from the prejudices of mainstream society. A significant segment of the population continues to lead broken or shattered lives, battered lives, lives without hope for the future. Social work, as a profession, appears to be largely stymied by these problems.

By offering aid to a variety of client populations, such as the disabled, the unemployed, the poor, the ill, the elderly, social work reinforces the impression that the organized society – the state – and its institutions care about and care for all the people within its confines. Yet, in my opinion, many social problems are aggravated or, indeed, created by the political, economic, and social conditions organized under the wide-ranging umbrella of the state – which then turns around and offers social work assistance.

All of this is not to say that for social workers themselves there is no job satisfaction. In fact, very few social work jobs provide a totally negative experience. Social workers might help a pensioner write up a claim for a financial supplement that eventually results in more money for her. We might help a child develop a better understanding of a difficult family situation or the inner strength to cope more effectively with a specific type of stress. We might listen to a lonely hospital patient express fears and doubts about the future, and be thanked for taking the time to listen. There is for some a kind of straightforward personal satisfaction in skilfully navigating the perilous route of red tape necessary to achieve a client's goal.

These satisfactions keep social workers going, but they also serve to shield us from our more critical feelings. Similarly they can shield us from analysing the role played by social agencies themselves in creating our powerlessness. Sometimes these satisfactions – not to mention the basic economic benefits of holding a steady job in a "worthwhile" profession – work to divert us away from the total, more disturbing, picture.

The Roots of the Social Work Crisis

Many front-line social workers feel alienated from their work, with a sense of powerlessness and frustration. There is low morale, unsupportive management. As one worker said about her colleagues, *If you ask any of these workers about how they see the future, they'll all tell you the same thing – I want to get the hell out of here.*

Conditions of work often militate against "getting the job done" – even if that were possible under the best of conditions. Why is this so? Why is it that social agencies, which have been established for the purpose of helping, end up by being part of the problem? Has the profession failed to deliver on its promises? Is Canadian society really serious about its aid to its own citizens? If we really want to help people, shouldn't we also tackle some of the root causes of social problems?

My short response to these questions is that social work is often used to paper over the cracks that have appeared over the years in the walls of an unjust society. As a result the major source of many social problems remains untouched. Typically social workers are expected to confine themselves to working with symptoms only.

To study – and, I hope, answer – some of the questions surrounding social work, this book will look at early attitudes towards "helping", and the emerging role of the welfare state; at who social workers are and how they are educated; at the work they do, in theory and practice, at how this work is organized, and at the people it affects – the "clients"; and finally, at some alternatives to the present way of doing things.

The hierarchical nature of social work organization as it now operates means that clients almost always come lowest in the pecking order. This book means to give clients a stronger voice – at the expense, justifiably, of social workers and the dominant "professional" voice of institutional management.

The other important theme that will thread its way through this study is that the principles, management, and practice of social work are distorted – subverted – by structural conditions that have their roots nourished by the dynamics of gender, racism, and economic class. To begin with, most social workers come from the middle class and are educated to be "professionals". Most social workers have also traditionally been women, and this has had its effects on the status, organization, and control of the work. Women social workers, as Jennifer Dale and Peggy Foster point out in their book *Feminists and State Welfare*, "have never exercised control over their profession nor over those organizations in which social work takes place".[2]

At the same time most clients are the poor and dispossessed: the unemployed or underemployed, or the unemployable, the young and displaced, the elderly, the disabled. Most of these people again are women. Many of the clients are people of colour (once again with a majority of women). If a sense of powerlessness afflicts social workers, that sense is magnified greatly in the case of clients.

Why such a situation remains unchanged is directly linked to why a state chooses to maintain questionable institutions rather than to change them. Despite the much-touted freedom of choice that we are supposed to enjoy, it is dramatic how un-free our thinking is, especially when we probe the causes for the powerlessness and despair experienced by a large segment of the population. There is ample support for inquiries into the "pathologies" of the poor and the troubled, their personality deficits, their family stress, or their childhood traumas. Yet at the same time there is a strong taboo against asking: To what extent are unemployment, poverty, and basic inequalities directly or indirectly traceable to decisions made by a small group of people who possess the most power and wealth in the society?

Social Work and Social Structure: The Invisible Walls

The public has all along been encouraged to accept the welfare state as benign – that it is society's attempt to provide a minimum income and a "range of social services" for *all* members of society, that it attempts to reduce economic insecurity resulting from such "contingencies" as sickness, old age, and unemployment.[3] However, there is also another view. As Ian Gough points out, the welfare state:

> simultaneously embodies tendencies to enhance social welfare, to develop the powers of individuals, to exert social control over the blind play of market forces; and tendencies to repress and control people, to adapt them to the requirements of the capitalist economy. Each tendency will generate counter tendencies in the opposite direction; indeed, this is precisely why we refer to it as a contradictory process through time.[4]

Such a contradictory process is viewed by many social scientists as stemming from the requirements of a patriarchal and capitalist society and its dominant ideology. When the ownership and control of production and reproduction along with power in political and cultural institutions are confined to one gender and a small group of white people – whether they're called the corporate elite, the ruling class, or the rich (and famous) – the system creates and maintains its own built-in, ineradicable inequalities. Viewed in this light, the institutions of the welfare state are the dominant system's attempt to gloss over the very inequalities it creates in the first place.

Despite the welfare state and its social workers, ostensibly working for the well-being of the entire population, the system's distribution of power and resources remains profoundly unequal between men and women, between whites and non-whites, and between the economic classes. On the contrary, power has continued to further concentrate among the already-powerful. The richest one-fifth of Canadians control 71 per cent of the nation's wealth; the poorer two-fifths hold only 0.7 per cent.[5]

This unequal distribution of wealth has its human costs. One study comparing the lowest income group in Canada with the highest concludes that if you come from the lowest income group your life expectancy is six years less if you are male, and three years less if you are female. If you come from the lowest income group your chance of heart disease is twice as high. You can expect an infant mortality rate that is 1.95 times higher for male infants and 1.86 times higher for female infants.[6]

In his groundbreaking book *The Vertical Mosaic*, published in 1965, sociologist John Porter recognized the role of class and gender in economic decision-making. He argued that economic power was concentrated in the hands of a small group of men he designated as the "economic elite". He also illustrated the role of sex and racism in this organization of power.

> In every society there are established mechanisms by which members are sorted out and assigned to particular social tasks. Often this process is based on biological or inherited characteristics. In most societies there are, for example, male and female roles. Sex has always been an initial basis of sorting and assigning people to their appropriate tasks. Hence, in this particular society, few women occupy positions of power because it is not "appropriate" that women should. Colour is another important biological characteristic which has been used as a basis of sorting people out.[7]

This sorting out process is shaped by patriarchy – the systemic dominance of men over women through established social structures and social relations. This domination affects the treatment of women not only in society generally, but also more specifically in the production of wealth, and in the reproduction of new generations of human beings. Canadian sociologist Jane Ursel, for instance, defines patriarchy as "a system or set of social relations which operate to control reproduction through the control of women both in their reproductive and productive labour".[8] Dorothy Smith, widely recognized in Canada for her contributions to feminist theory and methodology, adds:

> We have come slowly to the discovery that gender permeates all aspects of social, political and economic organisation; that what has been seen as not gendered is in fact largely an exclusively male arena

of action and that from that viewpoint, gender relations are only present when women are. But from the standpoint of women, we are coming to recognise the pervasive effect or presence of gender.[9]

Another feminist theorist, Margrit Eichler, explains that one obvious reason for the relative invisibility of housework in our society is that the patriarchal family is the operative model for social organization. This means that the woman is defined as being economically dependent on her husband, and this has had an impact on her work within the home:

> Her work is, therefore, by implication seen as economically valueless, no matter what it may consist of and how much it would cost to replace it. Indeed this has been (and continues to be, to some degree) an explicitly accepted aspect of economic theory. In labour economics, the labour force is equated with gainfully employed workers, i.e. with paid labour.[10]

Patriarchy is also a force that goes far beyond our national boundaries. As a United Nations statement puts it:

> Women constitute *half* the world's population, perform nearly *two-thirds* of its work hours, receive *one-tenth* of the world's income and own less than *one-hundredth* of the world's property.[11]

These figures reflect a pervasive and persistent subordination of women to men, which is further complicated by other divisions of power within states. In *The Canadian Corporate Elite*, Wallace Clement took John Porter's work a step further by presenting detailed evidence showing that the various elites Porter saw as separate – the corporate, political, bureaucratic, church, intellectual – were in fact tightly linked and homogeneous, forming a "power elite".[12] Clement argued that this power elite determined the country's economic and political priorities and established its ideology through control of the mass media. This elite prevented the ideal of democracy from truly working in practice. It prevented Canada from fulfilling its promise of equal opportunity.

Clement stated that in a "liberal-democratic" state such as Canada, "The way society is organized provides some with the advantage to accumulate power and privilege then transfer these to their children in the form of wealth, stockholdings, social 'position', and access to education or 'inside' contacts for job placements."[13]

Granted that a dominant class largely influences our values, attitudes, and ideas. But there is more to domination than the inequalities of class. Feminist writers have cautioned us against viewing the mode of production as the sole force in the making of history and society. One contributor to Canadian feminist thought, Mary O'Brien, calls attention to the fundamental importance of reproduction as a mode of production ignored by "malestream" thought because it has to do with women as workers and producers, as key actors in production. O'Brien points out that while class analysis is important, it is clearly insufficient because it ignores the role of male supremacy:

> Reproductive relations, on the other hand, never do manage to make history in this interpretation.... This is pure patriarchal distortion; the act of biological reproduction is *essentially* social and human, and forms of the social relations of reproduction have as important an impact on the social relations of production as *vice versa*.[14]

O'Brien observes that gender conflict and class conflict produce forces for change which can be understood by analysing their different sources. She argues that the separation of the private life and the personal, on the one hand, from public life and the political on the other has come about through the historically developed structure of the social relations of reproduction: "The opposition of public and private is to the social relations of reproduction what the opposition of economic classes is to the social relations of production."[15]

It is important to recognize these differences in gender and class conflicts, as well as their common points. When we consider the multiple oppressions that are not only based on gender and class but also on racism, it is the experience of dominant / dependent social relations that applies in common.

This delineation of what I will call the "ruling class," in which power is wielded mainly by white males, is a complicated matter, involving intricate cross-currents of history, economics, ideology, gender roles, education, religion, the mass media – the list could go on and on. It can also be argued that because of foreign ownership of its economy, Canada has never had an independent ruling class: control of power has been complicated by a colonial relationship with, first, Great Britain, and more recently the United States.

The idea of white male authority within the ruling class is also not a matter of simple, mechanistic systems of conspiracy and domination. As media analyst Todd Gitlin puts it, "Society is not a machine or a thing, it is a coexistence of human beings who do what they do (including maintaining or changing a social structure) as sentient, reasoning, moral, and active beings who experience the world, who are not simply 'caused' by it."[16]

To explain why a population more likely opts for maintaining the prevailing institutions over trying to change them, Gitlin points to Antonio Gramsci's theory of *hegemony:* the "name given to a ruling class's domination through ideology, through the shaping of popular consent". According to Gitlin:

> Those who rule the dominant institutions secure their power in large measure directly *and indirectly,* by impressing their definitions of the situation upon those they rule and if not usurping the whole of ideological space, still significantly limiting what is thought throughout the society.[17]

As noted earlier, the same conditions of gross inequality replicate themselves on the international level. The discrepancy between the wealth of nations in North America and Europe, for instance, and those in the Third World has been well documented. The history of global colonialism is the history of racism, leaving a legacy of poverty borne primarily by non-white nations. A similar process has been at work in Canada where non-whites are victims of racial discrimination – in employment practices, in housing availability, in the inequality of education, to name a few blatant examples. Nowhere in the country have the social costs of institutionalized prejudice had a longer history than on Native reserves, where shockingly high rates of poverty, illness, and unemployment are recorded and where a sense of hopelessness has become an almost unavoidable way of life.

Although the terms prejudice, racism, and discrimination are often used interchangeably, Barb Thomas and Charles Novogrodsky summarize the differences in their book *Combatting Racism in the Workplace. Prejudice,* they point out, is a state of mind that, despite an absence of legitimate evidence, casts a group and its members in an inferior light. "Legitimate" means to be scientifically proven, and the lack of this proof means that prejudice is irrational. By contrast, *discrimination* is action or behaviour based on prejudiced attitudes. It results in the exclusion of certain populations from access to quality education, good jobs and promotions, decent housing, or participation in an organization. *Racism*, then, "is a form of discrimination. It is prejudice, plus the back-up of institutional *power*, used to the advantage of one ethnic group and to the disadvantage of other ethnic groups." Racism "subordinates people because of their colour or ethnicity".[18]

Although in recent years Canada's immigration laws have been modified, human rights commissions have been established, and the Constitution contains a bill of rights, University of Saskatchewan researchers B. Singh Bolaria and Peter Li have still concluded: "The evidence suggests that such changes have done little to ease racial tensions, much less resolve the problem of racism and discrimination."[19]

All of these factors – the role of gender and racism, of political and economic power and ideology, the uneven distribution of wealth and power – together create the social structures that dominate and confine our lives. These social structures are like invisible walls that accompany our every move, stretching on throughout our lives. The structures and relations of social work form one set of walls, for both worker and client. The larger structures and institutions of society – government, business, education, media, religion, family – form another set. Although these invisible walls do not by any means represent a unified system, they are closely linked, and together they take a heavy toll as we collide with them day in and day out and feel less and less certain about which way to turn.

A "welfare mother" expressed the sense of confusion – and anger – this experience creates:

> *My daughter and I are both anemic, so we should be buying vitamins but because I can buy them over the counter, welfare won't pay for them. I don't have the money so I said the hell with it! I've got a choice – either get the groceries I need or don't pay my bills. If I don't pay my rent, I'm out of my apartment. If I'm out of my apartment and can't find a place to stay, welfare will accuse me of being an unfit mother – and the government will take my kids. So what am I supposed to do?*

To get anywhere at all we have to first define and understand – locate – those invisible walls, and listen carefully and respectfully to the voices that manage to pierce through the cracks. Those voices provide their own analysis of how the society works. As a prisoner in jail told me:

> *In the schools I found there was no equality there. If you're the son of a coal miner, the teachers pay no attention to you; if you're the son of a doctor, they'll help you all they can. Most kids have some trouble with school work, but you're not helped as equals. You sure notice that when you're a kid. You get told by everybody to get A's. Then when you start getting all D's, that really does something to you. You get pushed to the back of the class and you feel you don't belong, that you shouldn't be there, you feel awful as a kid but you don't know what to do. It's very bad, you start going downhill.*

A young girl in a self-help group hesitantly described a different form of powerlessness:

> *The incest usually happened when my dad came home from the bar. He'd be drunk and he'd come into the room and like we'd be in bed most of the time when he came home, because we knew he'd be drunk. So we'd go to bed and he'd come into the room and he'd sit on my bed and he'd put his hands on my breasts and my privates and I'd just – I'd wake up and I'd be really scared. And upset about it. And I'd wonder, well, what's going to happen? I don't want this to happen – and then he'd climb under the covers and start committing the incest and I'd tell him to stop – that it hurt – leave me alone – that I didn't like it – but he just wouldn't go away.*

As painful as it might be, once we begin to listen, to talk, to see things more clearly, we can begin to start rebuilding, from the bottom up, rather than papering over the cracks.

The Challenge for Social Work

In Canada the evidence suggests that the welfare state has failed dismally in its promises for a just society. The role and practice of social work is symptomatic of this failure – and of the continuing human loss. Although as a social worker and a teacher of social work I am sympathetic towards at least some of the intentions – and some of the successes – of social work, I feel at the same time that it is vitally important to take a critical look at the role and practice of social work as a profession and as a method of intervention in society.

It is important that social work be challenged to become more democratically accountable. By democratic I mean the opening up of ways through which social programs can be subject to active review by those most closely affected: both clients and social workers. The general public must also have a role to play in this process, so that everyone involved will have a more effective voice in shaping the future.

Canadian society, unfortunately, does not place a high value on social services. And the term welfare state does not completely or adequately define the Canadian situation. Although the state contains a system of social welfare services, it also does many other things and, indeed, appears to place its priorities and its money elsewhere: on defence spending, or on building huge convention centres or domed stadiums, or on generally developing the necessary conditions for "investor confidence". The state often provides subsidies to industry out of taxpayers' money: "Corporate welfare bums" was the phrase the New Democratic Party's David Lewis used to describe these businesses. In other words, who really gets the public assistance?

A new form of intervention would call for a restructuring of our major institutions, so that they become answerable to the public rather than being strictly controlled by a relatively small class of people composed primarily of white wealthy males. Without such transformation those social problems now experienced will be perpetuated endlessly into the future, with bandaids being busily applied by a profession that should know better. The evidence for the need of such a transformation is in the following pages.

2

The Roots:
Early Attitudes

Mary Dowding 514 King St.E. and husband. No children. says can't get work. fancy they don't want it. no reason why they should be in want. Recommend a little starvation until self-help engendered, probably drink.

from notes of a volunteer visitor, Toronto 1882*

WHEN I WAS still a student in social work, the history of the welfare state was presented as a process of evolution whereby society gradually recognized its responsibility to the "less fortunate" or "underprivileged". Perhaps most Canadians also share this view about how social programs emerged. A closer examination, however, reveals a much different picture.

In fact, the professional relationship in social work – the historically developed link between help-giver and help-receiver – has been fraught with ambivalence from the earliest times. Historically the work of "charity" was a matter for churches and religious orders, whose teachings extolled the virtue of compassion towards

---

* Quoted in James Pitsula, "The Emergence of Social Work in Toronto," in *Journal of Canadian Studies*, vol. 14, no. 1, Spring 1979, p. 36.

the poor – while at the same time proclaiming that poverty was divine punishment for earthly sins. Compassion was key in the work of Vincent de Paul, who organized ways for people to visit the sick, the dying, the prisoners, and the poor in seventeenth-century France. The other side of the coin was state aid to the "needy", which took a decidedly punitive approach. It was as if needy people had committed a crime.

English law in 1531, certainly, was blunt about what would happen to the unemployed. A person considered to be one of society's ill-begotten group of "idle poor, ruffelers, sturdy vagabonds and valiant beggars" was "to be tied to the end of a cart naked and to be beaten with whips throughout the same market-town or other place til his body be bloody by reason of such whipping". As if this was not enough, this unfortunate would "also have the upper part of the grissle of his right ear clean cut off".[1] The poor in this case were far from being "blessed" in the eyes of the state.

At the same time as brutality was inflicted on jobless men, women were persecuted for being suspected of witchcraft. The accusation was focused mainly on spinsters and widows (that is, those women without male "protection") who might try to achieve a degree of personal independence. In doing this they posed a threat to the monopoly of male authority in intellectual, moral, economic, and spiritual spheres. Mary Daly documents the belief current in 1486 that "All witchcraft comes from carnal lust which is in women insatiable".[2] This belief, combined with the suspicion that some women were in league with the devil, served to justify witch-hunts and the subsequent torture and killings of large numbers of women.[3]

In time English law softened. Instead of being beaten and mutilated, the unemployed (or the "able-bodied" as they were called) were imprisoned and forced to work in jail-like institutions called houses of correction, "There to be straightly kept, as well in diet as in work, and also punished from time to time."[4] Influenced by the church, the state was somewhat less harsh to the "impotent poor", that is, the deserted mothers with children, the blind, the "lame", the "demented", the old, and the sick. These unfortunates could in seventeenth-century England receive limited assistance from officials who were called the "overseers" of the poor and who had been appointed to their positions by justices of the peace or magistrates. Two centuries later this division between worthy and unworthy poor remained, with both groups often ending up in workhouses or poorhouses, which had replaced the houses of correction. Charles Dickens attacked these workhouses in his novel *Oliver Twist*.

In Canada, governments imported the traditions of France and England. While Quebec's government left it to the Catholic church to provide assistance and education to the poor, the colonial administration in the Maritimes saw to the construction of a workhouse in 1759, where "for many years whipping, shackling, starvation, and other necessary inducements were used to correct the behaviour of the idle, vagrant, or incorrigible inmates".[5] There were also public auctions of paupers. In 1816 in the Upper Canada village of Delaware, an indigent widow was auctioned off to the *lowest* bidder.[6] What happened was that paupers were "boarded out" in a sort of foster-home system. The auction was to see who would charge the municipality *least* for their keep; the successful bidder would expect to more than make up his cost by work to be got out of the pauper.

Though workhouses were not developed everywhere in English Canada, the local jails served the same purpose: "Jails became a type of poorhouse – a catch-all for a variety of social problems – the homeless poor, the insane, the offenders, both petty and serious, young and old."[7]

In Europe some local governments gradually began collecting funds to distribute to needy men and women. This government involvement continued as the religious institutions found it impossible to keep up with the growing numbers who needed assistance. Public authorities, however, kept their aid to a bare minimum. This remained the case in Victorian England when religious and other charity groups proliferated to supplement government aid.

England in the nineteenth century had brutal factory conditions, including long hours of child labour. Trade unions were illegal, women had no vote, and living conditions of the working class were abysmal. The owners of industry and commerce felt that it was their superior moral character, not their economic structures, which was responsible for the widening gap between rich and poor, men and women, whites and non-whites. Such was their smugness, that some of the well-to-do genuinely felt that the pauper class needed only proper moral instruction to be raised out of their woeful condition.

If men had few rights during this era, women were seen as chattels, or as the property of men, with no separate existence of their own. Pat Thane summarizes:

> If the husband entered the workhouse, the wife would have no choice
> but to follow. A destitute wife could be refused entry to the work-
> house if her husband would not enter, or [could be refused] permis-
> sion to leave if he would not leave. If a male pauper was officially
> classified "not able-bodied", so was his wife, whatever her personal
> physical condition.[8]

Just as the position of the poor was a subordinate one, the same was
true of non-whites. During an age when many people still supported
slavery, there were ample theories to justify assumptions about the
superiority of the upper class and indeed of the growing middle
class, and the "natural rights" of the men in these classes to subordinate others.

One form of justification was the growing emphasis on
"scientific thinking", which by the nineteenth century was used to
explain why people occupied different ranks and status. Theories
such as the survival of the fittest, with arguments about the extinc-
tion of certain animal species and the continuation of other species,
were applied to thinking about people and economic status. Aristo-
cratic men, as a consequence, were viewed as the "fittest", possessing the most desirable of human traits. This group of "superior"
beings included men rather than women, whites rather than non-
whites, the physically healthy rather than the sick, property owners
rather than servants. The evidence for the aristocracy's "moral
superiority" was, presumably, their extraordinary wealth and their
ability to have their commands carried out.[9]

Conversely, it followed that the poor and the powerless possessed the least desirable traits. Those who were paupers, either due
to illness or physical disability, old age, low-paying jobs or unemployment, became viewed as "inferior" – a designation still very
much with us to this day.

Social progress was seen as the promotion of the most desirable
of human traits. Since the traits of the poor were considered not
worth preserving, it was logical for Thomas Malthus, writing in the
early nineteenth century, to conclude that no aid whatsoever should
be given to the have-nots. He felt that if all relief were withheld, the
poor would either develop proper moral qualities to equip them for
survival, or they would die. In short, the poor, Malthus argued,

should be abandoned and "nature" allowed to take its course. True, mass death would follow, but such a fate would be borne by the poor as "evils which were absolutely irremediable, [which] they would bear with the fortitude of men, and the resignation of Christians".[10]

While such prescriptions may have sounded perfectly "natural" to those who possessed abundant wealth, they were not exactly welcomed by the potential victims. In any case these more extreme ideas and programs were not implemented because most of the poor (including, especially, women and children) were needed and exploited as factory workers. Their labour was indispensable to the very same system that was keeping them poor. And with servants and women in the private sphere, the sexual and domestic servicing of their masters made the Malthusian logic too ludicrous to be acted upon.

The brutalities of the workhouses in England brought agitation for change by the working class and reformers in England. But a Royal Commission, established in 1834 to study the conditions of the poor, strongly recommended the continuation of workhouses for the poor, including the continuation of their harsh conditions. The reason they gave: We must protect work discipline. The Commissioners argued that without the harshness of the workhouse, the lowest-paid workers would lose their incentive to work:

> Their industry is impaired, their employment becomes unsteady, and its remuneration in wages is diminished. Such persons, therefore, are under the strongest inducements to quit the less eligible class of laborers and enter the more eligible class of paupers.[11]

In other words, if governments were to provide adequate aid the lowest-paid workers would quit their jobs and become eligible for public assistance. The Report went on: "Every penny bestowed, that tends to render the condition of the pauper more eligible than that of the independent laborer, is a bounty on indolence and vice."[12] The Royal Commission believed it had discovered a way to both aid the needy and protect the system. It would accomplish this by extending benefits to the poor at a level that was clearly less than the wage of the poorest-paid employee. There was to be no room for questioning whether the lowest wage was a fair wage. The net effect was to legitimate these lowest wages by focusing on the incentive of the working poor. In addition, this approach also created the illusion of freedom. The poor were to be given a "choice". Either work at abysmal wages or enter the workhouse.

To implement that Report, 600 more workhouses were built throughout England between 1834 and 1850.[13] It was the kind of thinking, fashioned by men of privilege, that still haunts our social welfare institutions and affects the ways that helping professionals see their work and their relations with clients.

Social Work: The Beginnings

In the late nineteenth century, when social work began as an embryonic profession in London, the main movers of charity accepted the established division between worthy and unworthy poor. There was a certain sympathy for the worthy poor, but for the unworthy – the able-bodied poor or the unemployed – it was still felt that the full rigour of the workhouse should be applied. Welfare state expansion tended to focus on these unworthy poor, often women: "unwed" mothers, "promiscuous" ladies, "irresponsible" wives, and so on. This left the worthy to be aided by the more traditional charitable organizations, outside the purview of the state.

The idea of more systematic social assistance took on an added sense of urgency when the affluent class noticed that socialism was becoming more appealing to their factory workers. Furthermore, the rich donors resented being pestered for donations to the many separate charities. Along with this resentment, there was the suspicion that many paupers were lying about their circumstances in order to collect more relief from more than one charity.

As a result, a new organization was formed in 1869 in London: the Society for Organizing Charitable Relief and Repressing Mendicancy. It was soon renamed the Charity Organization Society (C.O.S.). It offered to co-ordinate the various charities and advocated a thorough investigation of each application for charity. Such co-ordination and investigation came to symbolize "scientific charity", which borrowed ideas from the emerging social sciences and from factory management. With these innovations, charity leaders held out the promise of imposing efficiency upon the charity process. Through investigation of applicants, fraudulent claims would be weeded out. And for the truly needy, the cause of their poverty would be discovered.

The C.O.S. approach became popular and spread to other locations. At the operational level, the C.O.S. provided "friendly visitors" from the upper class, women who volunteered to visit poor families. So much importance was placed on developing a cooperative, helpful relationship between the help-giver and the help-receiver that it was the relationship itself which came to be viewed as the best form of assistance to the poor. Not that these well-off philanthropists expected the pauperized masses to rise above their wretched state. The goal of friendly visiting was to provide paupers with a life of dignity but within the confines of their continuing poverty. And since the C.O.S. leaders believed that financial aid would be wasted on the poor, their motto became "Not alms, but a friend."

The very organization of the C.O.S. reflected the subordinate position of women:

> Despite the fact that most of the visitors who assessed the means and morals of the poor were women, the leading figures who controlled the COS were predominantly men – Octavia Hill was indeed the only woman on the first council. Nevertheless, men were happy to inaugurate areas of work for women where they could in effect be the help-mates of men.[14]

Conveniently, for rich white men at least, this solution to poverty's problems was inexpensive. It also nicely camouflaged the connection between their growing wealth and the subordinate status of women, poor men, and non-white unfortunates. Happily for the rich, friendly visitors confirmed their own views about being superior mortals and gave them a clear conscience about their relationship to the poor.

In the late nineteenth century the C.O.S. was transplanted to North America.[15] The following advice was given to friendly visitors on how to develop co-operative, helpful relationships with the poor:

> You go in the full strength and joy and fire of life; full of cheer and courage; with a far wider knowledge of affairs; and it would be indeed a wonder if you could not often see why the needy family does not succeed, and how to help them up.[16]

Given the assumption that the poor were morally inferior, it was logical that assistance became defined as moral advice on how to uplift the poor into becoming better individuals. It was conceded that as time went on morally uplifted individuals might even escape their poverty.

Throughout this period the personal link between help-giver and help-receiver was maintained even while the message shifted from the previous religious uplift to moral uplift. With the emergence of social work, the content of the message would change again, but the centrality of the relationship between professional and client would remain.

Social workers, however, did not directly replace the well-to-do volunteer. There was an intermediate step, stemming from the nature of the C.O.S. Again, at the operational level, the C.O.S. format consisted not only of wealthy volunteers; but it also consisted of paid employees called "agents" who were often from the working class.[17] These "agents" were poorly paid and low status technicians. Initially they were few in number but as the quantity of cases grew and far exceeded the number of volunteers, more agents were hired and carried larger parts of the workload. This group of employees was the forerunner of the modern social worker.

In Canada the C.O.S. influenced how charity was dispensed during the nineteenth century. For example, in Toronto, before someone could receive charity (fuel or groceries) from the municipality's main charity organization, a visitor went to the applicant's home and conducted an investigation. These visitors were volunteer business and professional men who recommended whether to grant or withhold relief. As seen from the comfortable position of the visitor, poverty could be avoided by anyone who really wanted to. The "help" offered often consisted of withholding material aid. This punitive approach was rejected by the early social workers who took over from the volunteers in the 1910s and 1920s.

Many of these early social workers were women who were finding an outlet for their creative energies outside the home. Yet they found themselves answerable to wealthy male philanthropists or politicians. The result, according to Jennifer Dale and Peggy Foster, was that "The new professions were made up of middle-class women who were very much involved in the social control of working class mothers."[18]

This social control was reflected in the attitudes of Canada's early social workers. Although less punitive than the friendly visitors, they did not support the idea of government increasing financial aid to the poor. In the 1920s and 1930s Canadian social workers opposed measures such as family allowances out of a fear that the result would be an increase in the family size of an "undesirable" class of people. As one social worker stated at the time, people who earned low wages were "frequently physically and mentally unfit" and therefore certainly not to be trusted.[19]

The model adopted in social work, as social historian Terry Copp puts it, was "stern charity, charity designed to be as uncomfortable and demeaning as possible".[20] Copp analyses the case of Montreal, which in 1901 was home to a great variety of charitable institutions organized along ethnic and religious lines: "fifteen houses of refuge, thirteen outdoor relief agencies, fourteen old age homes, eleven orphanages, eighteen 'moral and educational institutions,' and more than a score of other miscellaneous charitable agencies."[21]

Most thinkers on social questions at the time thought that the proper role of the state was to be minimal – to maintain public institutions for the insane, the criminal, and the "absolutely unfit". Those who were simply poor or unemployed or "handicapped" in some way were to be left to the charitable institutions or, more likely, to their own devices. The prevailing attitude was that most of the poor who, for instance, resorted to begging were out-and-out frauds, and that it was in fact harmful to aid these people. The C.O.S. stated in its aims in 1901 that it wanted to focus its ideals on "the charity which is far and away above mere relief, the charity which means an uplifting of the whole tone of life". Relief should be given "only when it does good and not harm", and "the welfare of souls and characters is of more concern than freedom from physical suffering".[22]

Along the same lines, when the Depression created massive unemployment in the 1930s, social work leaders were suspicious of granting relief payments to the poor. One leader, Charlotte Whitton, argued that instead of money being paid to needy parents, children should be removed from their homes. She believed that many of the mothers were unfit as parents, and so: "The dictates of child protection and sound social work would require cancellation of allowance, and provision for the care of the children under guardianship and authority."[23]

Despite such resistance by many social workers, the expansion of the welfare state occurred in Canada due to several converging factors. The dislocation during and after the First World War – with the need for support both of injured soldiers and of families left behind – brought some initial forays into expanding state intervention. A greater force was increasing labour turmoil and worker dissatisfaction with brutally unfair conditions, as the urban population grew and industrialization continued. In the first three decades of the century, Terry Copp writes:

> All of the accepted norms of society were being called into question by the growing complexity and disorder of the industrial system. Montreal was being transformed into a sprawling ugly anthill. Frequent strikes and the growth of labour unions seemed to foreshadow class warfare on a European scale.... The fundamental social problem was poverty, massive poverty, created by low wages and unemployment. For individuals, direct assistance limited hunger and prevented starvation, but the small section of the working class which regularly came into contact with organized charity was too often confronted with the "alms of friendly advice" and too seldom helped to achieve security.[24]

In 1919 Winnipeg experienced a general strike when 30,000 workers left their jobs to fight for the principle of collective bargaining, better wages, and the improvement of working conditions. In this case the state proved only too eager to intervene, refusing to talk with unions but sending in Mounted Police and federal troops. The state clearly came down on the side of the manufacturers, bankers, and businessmen, and revealed a distinct distaste for ideas and actions involving workers' rights.

Police forces were also used against the institutions of indigenous people – who were portrayed as savages lacking in culture and possessing no worthy structures of their own in the first place. The House of Commons Special Committee on Indian Self-Government offered an illustration of this in its 1985 report:

> The Iroquois (as they were known by the French) or Six Nations (as the English called them) or the Haudenosaunee (*People of the Longhouse*, as they called themselves) have a formalized constitution,

which is recited every five years by elders who have committed it to memory. It provides for a democratic system in which each extended family selects a senior female leader and a senior male leader to speak on its behalf in their respective councils. Debates on matters of common concern are held according to strict rules that allow consensus to be reached in an efficient manner, thus ensuring that the community remains unified. A code of laws, generally expressed in positive admonitions rather than negative prohibitions, governs both official and civil behaviour....

The Canadian government suppressed the Haudenosaunee government by jailing its leaders and refusing to give it official recognition. In 1924, the council hall at the Six Nations Reserve was raided by the Royal Canadian Mounted Police (RCMP). All official records and symbols of government were seized and have never been returned.[25]

With the Depression of the 1930s, working-class militancy spawned a series of protests, including the famous On-To-Ottawa Trek where 4,000 angry workers marched across Canada to present their grievances to parliament. Left-wing political groups were openly calling for an end to capitalism.

As a result of these kinds of opposition, leading industrialists began to grant concessions. Reluctantly they supported some expansion of the state into social welfare, provided it was understood that capitalism itself would not be threatened. Sir Charles Gordon, president of the Bank of Montreal, wrote to Prime Minister R.B. Bennett in 1934 to support the idea of unemployment insurance: "May I suggest to you that for our general self-preservation some such arrangement will have to be worked out in Canada and that if it can be done soon so much the better."[26] Not everyone in power agreed, but enough of them were persuaded to endorse an expansion of social welfare. When the federal government decided it was time to adopt unemployment insurance and other social programs, the same Prime Minister reminded business leaders why an expansion of the welfare state was necessary:

A good deal of pruning is sometimes necessary to save a tree and it would be well for us to remember there is considerable pruning to be done if we are to save the fabric of the capitalist system.[27]

To further camouflage this "pruning" of the capitalist system, business and government officials began to argue that our civilization had developed a capacity for compassionate responses to the needy, that "humane values" constituted the foundation of Canadian society, and that social programs were the manifestations of the society's concern for helping one's "fellow man" (they were perhaps less certain about women).

Within this rationale, political support was consolidated for Canada's social security programs. The first old age pension was introduced in 1927. Its payment of $20 a month was subject, as Dennis Guest puts it, "to a strict and often humiliating means test – proof that poor-law attitudes still influenced Canadian political leaders in the 1920s".[28]

In following years, workers' compensation for injuries, public assistance, child welfare, and public health programs were created or expanded. The 1950s and 1960s saw a substantial growth in social programs, with the federal government playing a key role in the funding of new, universal, old age security payments, an expanded unemployment insurance program, an evolving medicare approach, and additional social services geared to low-income Canadians.

The numbers of social service workers expanded at the same time, from 1,767 in 1941 to almost 28,000 in 1981.[29] This growth was in turn a response to the new sense of guiding "humane values" and of the need for a "modern" nation to make steady progress towards a just society. Social workers, it was said, viewed themselves as having an essential role to "ensure that citizens will have access to those materials, services and resources of society that will permit them to develop their potential as individuals."[30]

Critics, however, have a different point of view. They argue that the development of beliefs about helping are expressions of the system rather than challenges to it, that the welfare state was and is shaped by capitalism, sexism, and racism. One team of social work researchers states:

> Male supremacist ideas influenced the lines along which capitalism developed. To preserve the basis of male supremacy in the family it became necessary for men to discriminate against women in the labour market. Women became a vulnerable and manipulatable segment of the labour force used in factories.[31]

These researchers also argue that "Forms of discrimination against Blacks and women in the employment sector are similar":

> Both groups are confined to low-skilled, low-paying jobs, wage differentials for similar work, separate lines of seniority and advancement, exclusion from managerial and supervisory jobs, etc. All of these can be seen as methods of keeping each group in its "proper place".[32]

Women's inferior status in the labour force and elsewhere made them prime candidates for hardship and subsequent social work help. Paradoxically, nourishing others and helping were seen as female qualities, so that social work was undervalued but nevertheless tolerated. Even this toleration evaporates in the history of white society's relations with indigenous communities – where relations appear to be more a matter of social control than help.

But services provided by the state are more than a means of social control. They also represent battles fought and won over the years by working people. The welfare state stemmed in part from a militant labour movement and a consequent fear of revolution that prompted concessions to a population needing to be convinced that capitalism was capable of caring for its social casualties and of curbing its worse excesses. In this sense the welfare state played the role of legitimizing a political and economic system under attack.

One early critic, U.S. community organizer Saul Alinsky, argued 40 years ago that social workers

> come to the people of the slums under the aegis of benevolence and goodness, not to organize the people, not to help them rebel and fight their way out of the muck – NO! They come to get these people "adjusted"; adjusted so they will live in hell and like it too.[33]

An extreme view, perhaps, but one shared by many critics who see the traditional values of the past – the values of the poor laws for example – simply perpetuated under the guise of modern professionalism.

The new forms of social assistance represented, as Terry Copp puts it, the middle class's attempt "to devise plans to re-organize society without altering any of the fundamental economic relation-ships".[34] In the process the middle class not only assured a measure of gainful employment to some of its members but also, through the emergence of this new profession, social work, seemed to offer indisputable proof that we do live in a caring and just society.

3

Schools of Altruism

Social workers are dedicated to the welfare and self-realization of human beings; to the development of resources to meet individual, group, national and international needs and aspirations; and to the achievement of social justice for all....

Canadian Association of Social Workers, *Code of Ethics*

AN IMMENSE EMPHASIS on altruism pervades social work. Most students who enter social work have a strong desire to help others. In Canada some 4,000 students a year attend 26 schools of social work,[1] and as a reason for choosing their course of study they frequently say, "I want to help people." There is a selfless quality that views the client's needs as priority for action.

This apparent concern for the needs of others, for caring, pervades much of the material taught in schools of social work and becomes part of the informal culture among students. This idealism was very much part of my own experience when I was a social work student at McGill University. Like other students there I felt a certain scorn for one classmate who said he was "curious" about human suffering, but then showed no obvious desire to do anything about it. His curiosity may have been real enough, but we wondered what on earth he was doing in social work. We had certain expectations about how a social work student should think, and act.

Why do students decide in the first place to enter this or any other profession aimed at helping others? In some cases it is a matter of personal values: You have grown up with, or have adopted, a set of values that makes "helping others" important. The values might come from religion, politics, or simply from personal or cultural experience. They often spring from class differences. In some instances students see social work as a welcome chance to change direction in their lives, to do something "socially responsible". They might be responding to personal guilt, a sense that they have had a good life and it is time to give something back to society. Sometimes the personal experience of emotional pain leads to a desire to join a profession that promises to reduce such pain in its clients.

In my own case, I was a foster child at the age of five and later adopted. My childhood years were filled with a mixture of stress and love and I somehow managed, I think, to keep my sense of balance: so much so that in later years I was frequently able to offer emotional support to others. When I entered social work I felt that I had found a haven of sanity in a world filled with problems and injustices. Here seemed to be a corner that was "concerned", from which "professionals" could do something about stress, poverty, alcoholism, and despair.

In general most students who go into social work can be defined as middle class, both in respect to their financial resources and to their attitudes. University education is expensive and loans and scholarships are usually in short supply. As a result people with limited financial resources find it difficult to even consider going to university in the first place. Those who do go may find it difficult to complete their degrees.

In addition middle-class attitudes mean that most students and professors view the system as acceptable and as working well for themselves and most people. There are exceptions to this of course, but as a rule schools of social work see themselves turning out people who will be able to fit well into the social agencies after graduation. Minor criticisms of social agencies and of training courses are tolerated, even welcomed. But there is also a high premium placed on the student being able to carry out assignments with a minimum of conflict and dissatisfaction.

Most social work students and teachers used to be female. There was a marked shift in this after World War II and, as professor Joan Turner points out:

> By the later 1960s and the early 1970s, social workers were keenly working to improve their status as professionals, looking to medicine, psychiatry and law as models of successful (and, of course, male-based) professions. Without much thought to the sexism inherent in the move, schools of social work sought to recruit more male students and more male faculty. It was anticipated that the presence of more highly educated (Ph.D.) male educators in social work would enhance the status of the schools in the eyes of the university administrators and in the communities.[2]

The effect reinforced the tendency for men to hold senior positions. Among the heads of Canada's schools of social work in 1986, 22 were men compared to 4 women. This outcome is consistent with the findings of the Task Force on the Status of Women established by the Canadian Association of Schools of Social Work. The Task Force found there was a pattern of discrimination against women in the social work profession. More specifically, it found that women in schools of social work across Canada earn less, receive fewer promotions, and enjoy less job security than do their male counterparts.[3]

Racism has similarly influenced social work education. Despite efforts in some cases to recruit indigenous people into schools of social work, the numbers of Native social work students and faculty are lower than their proportion in the general population. This resistance against including non-whites is consistent with the findings from a study of U.S. social work educators, which revealed that black faculty perceived themselves as getting less respect and job satisfaction than white faculty.[4] In that same study the female black faculty members reported the lowest job satisfaction, illustrating what happens when the prejudices against gender and colour are combined.

Despite the inequalities in their structures, schools of social work continue to attract students who genuinely want to become professional helpers. This attraction is common to other human service professions. Whether it is nursing patients back to health or teaching children to read and write, or understand algebra, a deep sense of satisfaction often comes from one person helping another. Some researchers suggest that altruism has a biological basis and that mutual aid may be as much an instinct towards survival as the need to locate food.[5]

Psychoanalyst Erich Fromm, differentiating between selfishness and self-love, offers another approach. According to Fromm, selfish people are interested only in themselves, want everything for themselves, feel no pleasure in giving but only in taking. By contrast, self-love allows you to love and care for others, as you do for yourself. Caring for others can provide an ultimate meaning to life: "The affirmation of one's own life, happiness, growth, freedom, is rooted in one's capacity to love," Fromm writes. And, "Giving is more joyous than receiving, not because it is a deprivation, but because in the act of giving is the expression of my aliveness."[6] Perhaps because such "giving" does strike a responsive chord, it has become fashionable to advertise the "helpful" side of our major institutions. And so we hear about the "helpful" bank offering to arrange our loans or about nuclear weapons "helping" us to defend our borders.

What about social work help? What makes it unique? Teachers in social work often say our profession is concerned not only with an individual's well-being, but also with society's well-being. This definition provides a scope so wide that many students in their first year are immensely impressed. It is as if almost anything can be part of social work, providing it has a component of fostering personal or social well-being.

Schools of social work mix in material from psychology and psychiatric theory, offering a gateway to the world of personal motives, subconscious drives, family dynamics, pathological responses, and on and on. It is exciting stuff. Students can and do apply these concepts to themselves, their peers, and to others. But it doesn't end there. There's also the focus on the societal level. Materials and approaches from sociology, political science, and economics are selected, condensed, and applied to social welfare. Students learn about various social security schemes, law-making processes, and political pressures. Again, heady stuff. And with Canadian governments currently spending over $42 billion per year on income security programs, students quickly get the feeling they've arrived in the big league.[7]

This range of study only provides the foundation for what is usually deemed the "primary" area of social work training. In this primary area, attention is concentrated on training students to develop practical, professional skills. As students proceed with their training, their desire to help others becomes focused more strictly around acquiring practical skills. "I want to learn how I can conduct better interviews," says one. "I want to improve my assessment skills," says another. "I'd like to learn more about family therapy."

Most students want to learn how to do counselling with individuals and families. A minority have a major interest in research, agency administration, community work, or policy analysis. This reflects the reality of the job market. The majority of social work graduates become employed in the provision of direct services to individuals and families.[8] To tailor students for such jobs, social work training includes instruction on how to listen to and clearly understand what clients are saying, how to observe non-verbal cues, how to get clients to communicate their thoughts and, especially, their feelings. Such skills are sometimes referred to as "professional relationship skills". The importance of them to social work students has been articulated by a standard text:

> Social workers believe that the character or quality of a relationship is important in all kinds of human interaction, but particularly in that between client and worker. This is true regardless of the time of interaction or the size of the client system. A swift exchange of feeling is necessary to engender trust and engage the client system. This relationship is largely a result of input by the worker, whose attitudes, skills and knowledge will influence what the client thinks of the worker as a person and as a professional.[9]

With this emphasis on professional relationship skills, social work has zeroed in on the psychology of human interaction, although from time to time valiant attempts have been made to introduce political questions as a focus.

Students and the Historical Task

One of the early pioneers of social work education was Mary Richmond, who in the early part of the twentieth century urged the establishment of schools for the "profession of applied philanthropy". She wrote: "Mass betterment and individual betterment are interdependent, however, social reform and social case / work of necessity progressing together."[10] Her classic book *Social Diagnosis* (1917) did build upon the early practice of using volunteers to do the necessary work, but she also tried to remove some of the paternalistic biases that had taken hold.

Mary Richmond emphasized the importance of investigation, fact-gathering, and the application of methods of diagnosis and treatment to each particular case. Instead of social problems being seen as caused by "moral deficiency", they came to be seen as the individual's "adjustment deficiency", that is, the person's failure to adjust to his or her surroundings. The professional task became one of helping clients adjust to the existing state of affairs. Embellished with psychoanalytic theories, these teachings then grew into casework or clinical social work. Students were trained to develop therapeutically helpful relationships with their clients, a tradition that continues today within schools of social work.[11]

Aside from training students in relationship skills, social work educators are also placing an increasing emphasis on external environments as sources of social problems. For example, Carel Germain and Alex Gitterman use an ecological perspective in their approach to social work. They say their perspective "provides an adaptive evolutionary view of human beings in constant interchange with all the elements of their environments".

> Human beings change their physical and social environments and are changed by them through processes of continuous reciprocal adaptation.... If human beings do not secure the appropriate nutriment (input, stimuli, information, energy, resources) from the environment at the appropriate time, their biological, cognitive, emotional and social development may be retarded and their functioning impaired.... Put another way, people, like all living organisms, together with their environment, form an ecosystem in which each shapes the other.[12]

To social work teachers, the personal-environmental connection offers a welcome rebuttal to conservative opinion that places total responsibility on the individual while ignoring the role of the environment. This rebuttal also fits with social work experience, which has grown sceptical about the exaggerated claims made on behalf of rugged individualism. Now social work offers more than theory about the individual-environment interaction; professional training attempts to apply such theory to the teaching of social work skills – although in practice there remains an apparent emphasis on individual adjustment and responsibility.

Professor Lawrence Shulman in *The Skills of Helping Individuals and Groups* argues:

> Obstacles can easily obscure the mutual dependence between the individual and important systems. When both sides have lost sight of this important connection, a third force is needed to help them regain this understanding.[13]

For Shulman, the helping professions represent this third force. He adopts the view that social work functions to mediate the process through which "the individual and society reach out for each other through a mutual need for self- fulfillment".

The recent emphasis on a balance between the individual and external systems has historical roots, going back to the settlement house movement, which laid the foundation for social work's focus upon social conditions. The first Settlement House was founded in London in 1884 when its affluent sponsors encouraged university men to settle in the poorest districts of the city in order to provide a spiritual and social uplift to the neighbourhood. The approach appealed to young members of the upper class as a means of fulfilling their civic duty. But instead of attempting to uplift one individual at a time, the entire neighbourhood became the arena for change. This approach was quickly transported to North American cities, where philanthropists sponsored the establishment of settlements and downtown community centres.

In his research into U.S. charities of the nineteenth century, Roy Lubove found a basic fear expressed by the Charity Organization Society of New York in its 1887 Annual Report: "If we do not furnish the poor with elevating influences, they will rule over us by degrading ones."[14]

"There is now a general acceptance of the idea that the welfare state plays a key role in protecting the social stability of Western capitalist societies," writes Martin Loney, a teacher of community work.[15] Loney quotes Bryce Mackasey, a former Liberal Party cabinet minister, who stated bluntly to the elite Canadian Club in 1972 that "The stability of free enterprise depends on the welfare state".

Four years later the chief economist of Ford Motor Company observed that "Unemployment insurance and welfare are two reasons why there isn't blood on the streets" in Canada.[16]

Yet the paradox of such privilege-enhancing altruism is that it can lay claim to represent social progress as well. By permitting such distortion, social work education creates an image of the profession as being at the forefront of social progress and social change:

> At this crossroads of competing values stands the social worker with a double historical task of urging movement toward the social good and rescuing those who have been lost or trampled on in the mass competitive rush toward personal affluence and social upgrading. The social worker ideally represents the social conscience of the community, prompting us toward action in keeping with our highest ideals.[17]

The catch is the contradiction between being in a "profession" – with its accoutrements of developing a career, status, money, power, and so on – and being in this forefront. The truth is that more often than not social work has dragged its heels. For example, Goldwin Smith, who helped form Toronto's Associated Charities in 1888, became alarmed at what he felt to be unjustified demands for social security and more democracy: "No measure could be more thoroughly demagogic than this of Old Age Pensions. Payment of members, universal suffrage and female suffrage will probably follow. Then where will you and your Empire be?"[18] This commitment to the status quo was echoed by numerous social work pioneers. Edward T. Devine, a leader in developing the charity organization societies in the United States, said in 1918:

> When I seek with absolute frankness, and very earnest desire to see things as they are, the causes of misery here.... I have no more intention of changing the basis of our society, of our industry, or our civilization, than the physician intends to challenge the laws of anatomy or physiology, when he looks upon disease.[19]

Such attitudes were also typical in the early years of the Canadian Association of Social Workers when it preferred to remain aloof from taking public positions on social legislation. Even in the 1930s this association of professional social workers refused to make public comments on social issues. At a January 1932 meeting, one of the local branches of the Canadian Association of Social workers reported:

> Social workers are paid by the capitalist group, for the most part, in order to assist the under-privileged group. Thus organized support of political issues would be very difficult if not dangerous ... because of the danger of attempting too radical changes, since we are paid by the group who would resent such changes most.[20]

Since then, the Canadian Association of Social Workers has been somewhat less timid. But Elspeth Latimer's research into the Association from its inception up to 1966 leads her to conclude:

> We are nevertheless left with a pervasive feeling of uncertainty regarding the seriousness of the Association's commitment to bringing professional social work influence to bear on social affairs.... While many comments were made on social matters, the pursuit of causes in any on-going sense tended to be a rare occurrence.[21]

Nevertheless, by going beyond a focus on individual adjustment, social work opened the gate for its students to learn more about environmental factors. Most schools of social work located themselves within colleges and universities and were influenced by sociology and political science. The rise of social movements, such as the labour movement, civil rights movement, and feminist movement, illustrated how personal well-being was connected to the political process. The welfare state grew and social work educators expanded their sphere of interests.

Social Work and Systems Theory

Social work training needed a unifying theory or a framework that could make sense out of the variety of personal-environmental processes within the society. The answer, supposedly, was to be provided by systems theory.

Systems theory, now popular in social work textbooks, was developed by sociologists who had in turn adapted it from the physical sciences. According to the theory, individuals, families, neighbourhoods, workplaces, and other institutions are all examples of systems, all with their own boundaries within which they carry out their particular function. Each system is understood as being interdependent with the other systems that comprise its environment. By such means as inputs, outputs, and feedback with its environment, each system is viewed as striving to retain sufficient equilibrium to grow and change to better carry out its functions. In other words, the survival and development of social systems are seen as hinging on stability – which invokes a social control function, so that the various parts can be better "integrated" into the larger order. For social work, systems theory has also been used as a way to understand interactions between clients, workers, and their respective environments.

Systems theory appeared to be an advance in thinking because it discouraged social workers from giving exclusive attention to the internal psyche of individual clients. But despite its promise it contains several flaws. For one thing, it ignores the power gap between social work professionals and clients. U.S. critics of social policy Richard Cloward and Frances Fox Piven write:

> The systems theory approach invites social workers to view clients as "interacting" with a variety of "systems" in which we should ostensibly "intervene". The very blandness of the language denies any recognition of the realities of power. We learn that inmates "interact" with prisons; that mental patients "interact" with state mental hospitals; that recipients "interact" with welfare departments; that children "interact" with foster care agencies; that slum and ghetto dwellers "interact" with urban renewal authorities. But most clients do not "interact" with these systems, they are oppressed by them.[22]

The advocates of systems theory reply that their approach definitely allows for social change. They acknowledge that external systems (whether families, bureaucracies, or other institutions) may be inadequate because:

> (1) A needed resource system may not exist or may not provide appropriate help to people who need it, (2) people may not know a resource system exists or may be hesitant to turn to it for help, (3) the policies of the resource system may create new problems for people, or (4) several resource systems may be working at cross-purposes.[23]

But while the proponents of systems theory acknowledge defects within the specific *subsystems* of our society, these same proponents are careful to avoid any suggestion that it may be the entire system which is defective. In other words, their theory allows social work students to consider how to help change a specific subsystem, but the reconstruction of the entire system is considered out of bounds. Allen Pincus and Anne Minahan, after showing how to use systems theory within social work practice, argue: "It has been repeatedly demonstrated that society will not support any activity which has an objective of bringing about fundamental change in the very fabric of social institutions."[24]

The consequent aversion to basic change served to supplement the widespread fear that any extreme change in our society must lead to state dictatorship. By contrast, there is a different school of thought within social work, a perspective held by a minority of teachers who view the need for alternative structures to be based on the development of more democracy rather than less. This perspective also contains the yeast of altruism but it is a form of altruism recognizing that real help will be stifled so long as there are built-in structures of inequality within a given society.

At the operational level, this egalitarian approach to people – consumers and providers of service – attempts to redefine social work practice. Such redefinition integrates the personal and political aspects of social problems and their remedies. This approach retains the importance of relationships but believes that relationships flowing in hierarchical patterns (top-down) are as ineffectual as those based on assumptions of moral superiority. Feminist social workers are pioneering ways of using this alternative form of practice. Helen Levine of Carleton University's School of Social Work writes:

> Personal stress and distress are seen as a barometer, a kind of fever rating connected to the unequal and unhealthy structures, prescriptions and power relationships in women's lives. There is a rejection of the artificial split between internal feelings and external conditions of living and working, between human behaviour and structural context. A feminist approach to working with women involves weaving together personal and political issues as causes of and potential solutions to women's struggles. Women's troubles are placed within, not outside their structural context.[25]

Despite the possibilities contained in practice aimed at optimizing egalitarian relationships and structures, social work education usually prefers to emphasize the more conventional assumptions, such as: (1) Try to help your clients to adapt, to function "better", but, because social workers cannot by themselves produce social change, make no unrealistic claims about changing social conditions; and (2) even where it's feasible to change social conditions, the way to do it is through the political process and not through social work practices.

In this way the existing social structure is understood as "given". The professional task is then viewed as helping people as much as possible within the confines of present institutional arrangements. One student said:

> We are taught that "help" happens in the interaction between clients and systems. If we can strengthen that interaction, then things will get better. This doesn't deal with larger problems of inequalities and capitalism. We are taught to accept the larger structure.

Despite the tolerance of systems theory for some reform, the main emphasis of skills training is on the adjustment of the individual client or family to cope better within existing social conditions: shades of an earlier era.

So when government agencies establish their policies, procedures, and rules for providing aid to clients, social workers normally see it as their job to carry out these expectations. Similarly, students are trained to carry out what these agencies expect. This is one reason why there ends up being a fatal gap between social workers and the clients. For example, when clients were asked to address students at the University of British Columbia, one of them recalled:

> When we told students in social work about our experiences, they were stunned. They figured it's a rainbow out there and all they have to do is say to clients "I'm on your side." But it's not that easy. They were stunned to find that families on welfare were bitter, frustrated, and degraded. It seems to me they had never heard of the realities, that they just learn about policies. They didn't realize the strains, the hatred. Maybe they thought all clients liked social workers. They were surprised to hear about all those applications we're expected to

fill out, all the lecturing we get about getting jobs. They didn't know that the jobs we could get pay so poorly they don't even cover the costs of day care and transportation. From my experience, social workers don't get down to the core – why children on welfare are feeling the way they are. Social workers are fast to blame the family but they don't go to the roots of these frustrations. And a lot of it has to do with not having enough money.

Though being on welfare may be foreign to most students, this is not always the case. A small proportion of social work students do come from low-income families. Some have been through child welfare institutions. Some are physically disabled. A few belong to indigenous people, minority groups, and immigrant populations. Nevertheless, despite this mixture of backgrounds, the over-all tone in schools of social work remains one of aspiring to middle-class or higher status. A student reflected on this tone:

The school didn't deal with cultural differences or about differences in cultural attitudes. We didn't touch on Native, immigrant or refugee issues.... We are taught to work within the system and don't create too many waves or you'll be seen as unprofessional.

There is a prevailing approval of the status quo. I remember one school of social work Dean saying, "There's nothing wrong with our economic system because it has served the majority of Canadians very well."

When such attitudes permeate schools of social work, students tend to side with the social agency and its problems rather than with the clients. Many of them are in for a mixture of shock and confusion when they confront the conditions "outside":

I went to the welfare office. The waiting room smelled of urine. It was smoke-filled with no ventilation, a small room holding 80 people. The walls were kicked in. There were cigarette butts everywhere. I had to go through locked doors to get to the offices and I felt like I was a prisoner. When I asked about the locks, they told me the staff was threatened – if clients can't get their cheques some go berserk.... There was no dignity there. The place made you feel like scum. It was as if the whole structure was accepting it. When I talked about it with other students, they were concerned – but only for the staff. These students were not upset by it and were accepting of it. They were too caught up in carrying out their role in handing out cheques.

Social work's official aspirations of achieving social justice – and practical ideas for bringing this about – are not receiving priority, then, within schools of social work. Granted that the schools and their Deans are part of larger institutions and heavily influenced by the policies of universities and colleges. Nevertheless these schools also have some autonomy. Within their range of autonomy, values of social justice are often contradicted by the school's own practices.

By being part of the larger university or college, schools of social work are themselves subject to a host of rules and policies governing items such as fee schedules, grading criteria, and course design. The expectations to conform to these rules apply generally to university education, as do the pressures on professors to spend more time on research (and therefore less time with students). As a consequence the social relations between professors and students are usually experienced as impersonal and alienating. Furthermore, realizing the importance of good grades to their academic success, students have a strong incentive to feed back what professors want to hear.

More specific to professional training are the field-work courses that place students in social agencies as part of the curriculum. This practical component in social work education allows students to carry a small caseload of clients or to do other assignments that are part of professional practice. To successfully complete these courses students are highly dependent on the good will and attitudes of their field-work supervisors, who are typically employed by social agencies.

Students are assessed not only on how well they relate to clients but also on how well they respect the agency's mandate (and its limitations) and fit into the agency's work. Assessments of student performance are rooted in those social work theories that value "helping" clients adjust to existing conditions. Not that students are expected to issue directives for clients to follow. The process is far more subtle. Students are encouraged to ask about what clients want, to empathize with their problems, to explain what the agency can or cannot do, and to offer help only on terms acceptable to the particular agency. In this way students learn to replicate professional roles that provide help based on socially acceptable or officially defined options.

Students are taught that the best way to act upon their concerns is to develop their technical skills. They are also taught that by acquiring these technical skills, they will be capable of enhancing their clients' interpersonal relationships and enriching their clients' interactions with specific systems within our society. As a result, students develop an excessive faith in the power of their emerging technical expertise to overcome problems that are essentially of a political and structural nature. This type of confidence in professionalism has contributed to the growth of social work.

That growth has its critics. Ivan Illich argues:

> The disabling of the citizen through professional dominance is completed through the power of illusion. Religion finally becomes displaced, not by the state or the waning of faith, but by professional establishments and client confidence.... A profession, like a priesthood, holds power by concession from an elite whose interests it props up.... This kind of professional power exists only in societies in which elite membership itself is legitimized or acquired by professional status. Professional power is a specialized form of the privilege to prescribe.[26]

Illich points to what many people have suspected for some time: namely, that professions are self-serving even though they profess to serve others. While this may be more evident in professions like medicine and law where practitioners reap handsome incomes, similar dynamics operate in social work.

The sense of professional power is partly created, and certainly nourished, by the educational experience of social work students. It springs as well from history and from the prevailing political, economic, and social relationships. And in the end, in professional practice, the power relationships are firmly buttressed by the institutions and agencies that end up employing the graduates of social work schools.

4

Social Workers:
On the Front Line

The pressure of working with people in crisis is extremely draining. I had an excellent supervisor who understood this. She instituted a change which helped our morale. We'd work one day with clients and one day following up with paper and arrangements; the second day felt like a "day off" even though we were all working in terms of the paper follow-ups. But you knew the difference and as a result we became quite efficient. Then, I understand this supervisor got flak from the other managers. Before you knew it, we were back to every day seeing clients in crisis, with a new supervisor wanting 20-minute interviews.

a social worker, British Columbia

IF BOTH SOCIAL workers and their sense of altruism are under pressure, it is clear that as much – or more – of this pressure comes from above, from government, institutions, and managers, as from below, from the clients. Part of the pressure too has come from the unprecedented expansion of social work in the post-World War II era.

Membership in the Canadian professional social work association grew from 600 in 1939 to 3,000 in 1966 to over 9,000 twenty years later.[1] The profession has enlarged its operations in a host of new fields, ranging from gerontology to drug addiction, from child welfare to social security payments. The Canadian Association of Social Workers, in its *Code of Ethics,* states somewhat grandly:

> Social workers are engaged in planning, developing, implementing, evaluating and changing social policies, services and programs that affect individuals, families, social groups, organizations and communities. They practise in many functional fields, use a variety of methods, work in a wide range of organizational settings, and provide a spectrum of psychosocial services to diverse population groups.[2]

This tendency towards professional expansion has not proceeded without challenge. Governments wishing to justify cutbacks have accused social workers of drowning clients with an overabundance of services. They have been accused of doing too much for troubled families, thereby weakening the family as an institution.

Part of the pressure on social workers also comes from the role they adopt and practise – as professionals. The average salary levels for social workers are modest, but after all, money isn't everything. Social work's capacity to make professional judgements, to channel clients along one path instead of another, to offer advice to decision-makers about what social programs should be doing: These are elements of professional power. They are partly why we want to go into a profession, whether consciously or unconsciously. According to John McKnight:

> Professional services define need as a deficiency [in the client] ... As *you* [the client] are the problem, the assumption is that *I,* the professionalized servicer, *am the answer.* You are not the answer. *Your peers* are not the answer. *The political, social and economic environment* is not the answer. Nor is it possible that there is no answer. I, the professional, am the answer. The central assumption is that service is a unilateral process. I, the professional, produce. You, the client, consume.[3]

This criticism, however, overstates the extent of social work power while understating the extent to which professionals are serving power groups other than themselves. True, the social worker is in a stronger power position than the client. But social workers, like other professionals, are not a power unto themselves. Social work also exists as part of larger institutions, which are in turn shaped by larger forces.

Most social workers are employees of social agencies, which in turn are influenced directly or indirectly by the welfare state, and the practice of those agencies is an integral function of the welfare state. In Canada this welfare state includes a wide range of government commissions, departments, and agencies organized for the purpose of enhancing the public's general welfare – by which is meant our social as well as economic well-being. One way of promoting these goals is the deployment of social workers within agencies, both within and outside government.

The state itself does not take responsibility for all the country's social welfare needs. These needs – when they are met at all – are more likely funded by a combination of state and private sources and administered through para-public, trade union, church, and non-profit institutions.

Where Social Workers Work

Social workers find themselves plying their trade in a number of different ways. They may work in the voluntary (or private) sector for agencies such as the YWCA / YMCA, Elizabeth Fry Society, or John Howard Society. These agencies are governed by voluntary boards of directors made up of individuals who are often "prominent" and moneyed people in the community and who receive no direct remuneration for their activities on the boards. These boards in turn hire workers to carry out all or part of their programs.

Sometimes the voluntary agencies are established by religious and ethnic minority groups who raise their own funds to finance, for example, the Catholic Family Services, the Jewish Homes for the Aged, the Salvation Army, or the Caribbean Immigrant Services. Many of the agencies in the voluntary sector receive funding from donations collected through local charity appeals, such as the United Way. It is mainly from within this sector that much of social work evolved into a profession during the early part of the century. Increasingly, however, these agencies are also obtaining supplementary funding from government and are thus becoming more and more influenced by government policies and organization.

A small but growing number of social workers also work in private practice, running their own offices much as lawyers do, with clients paying fees for service. Or they work in the quasi-government sector, in settings that have voluntary boards and are partially autonomous as organizational structures, but are at the same time governed by state legislation and regulations, and have funding that originates from the state. Hospitals, which often employ social workers as part of their staff, fit into this category.

Perhaps the best-known examples of the quasi-government sector are the Children's Aid societies in Ontario, where social workers obtain their authority from provincial legislation. Each of Ontario Children's Aid societies, in different locales throughout the province, has its own volunteer board of directors, which establishes policies and standards for social workers to follow. (Most provinces, it should be noted, maintain child welfare agencies within the public sector, that is, operated directly as part of the government.)

But undoubtedly the largest single area for social work is in the government sector, with social workers employed directly by the welfare state. These social services carry out services that are often statutory. Their tasks and the decisions they make are specified by government regulations and policies. An example is public or social assistance – better known as "welfare" – which provides for the payment of limited amounts of money to people who have little or no financial resources. Social workers interview applicants for welfare, assess their needs, and decide whether the client qualifies for assistance based on the agency's regulations and policies. They sometimes provide counselling and various job training projects, mainly in large urban centres.

Each province has its own public assistance laws, regulations, and policies, though similarities do exist across the country. In Ontario, for example, it is the General Welfare Assistance Act and the Family Benefits Act. In Saskatchewan it is the Saskatchewan Assistance Plan. In New Brunswick it is the Social Welfare Act. Regardless of the province, the amounts received by welfare recipients still leave them so far below the official poverty line that to pay the rent means taking from the food money.

Though social work has often been equated with welfare or public assistance, there are numerous other agencies within the public sector where social workers are employed. A partial list includes probation services within juvenile and adult correctional branches, alcohol detox centres, mental health clinics and psychiatric services, and outreach programs for transient youth.

How Clients Find Social Workers

The needs that bring clients to a social work agency – or bring an agency to the client – are many and complex. The problems can range from wife battering to poverty, child abuse to alcoholism, drug addiction to marital strife, or conflicts in the paid workplace or at school.

If you've had a serious illness that prevents you from returning to your job, you might have to seek out a social agency to get financial help or advice. A patient in a hospital or a student having difficulty might be referred to the hospital's social service department or the school's social work counsellor. You could get a visit from a social worker if you are a parent and someone (a neighbour, teacher, or doctor) suspects you have violently abused your child and reports you to a welfare agency. If you have been convicted of a crime you might be ordered by the court to report to a probation officer, who is a social worker. The *official* message to clients is: we're here to help you.

If you are experiencing severe interpersonal problems (in your marriage, for instance) you might seek out social work counselling. That would probably bring you to a social agency in the voluntary sector. Or, you might find yourself going to a private practitioner's office.

In some cases it is the social agency that takes the initiative. The agency may identify individuals and families who it feels are most likely to experience social problems. This means, for the most part, the poor. In turn most of the poor are women and children. Rich people who need help can afford to use private services, and as a result their problems and needs remain more hidden.[4]

There is a marked contrast between a client voluntarily seeking help – say, with an alcohol problem – and an involuntary situation where a court compels the client to receive social services. A rough rule of thumb is that involuntary social services are provided by government agencies, whereas the voluntary sector tends to offer services that clients are free to accept, reject, or approach on their own initiative. Thus the term "voluntary" applies to more than the social agency's board. It can also apply to the level of client choice in accepting the social worker's services. To the degree that client choice is reduced, the welfare state moves in with its own definitions and solutions.

How Social Workers Mean to Help

Depending on the agency and on the client population, most social workers offer access to financial and other resources and provide various types of counselling. Providing access to resources might include helping a client get access to subsidized housing, searching out a decent nursing home for an ailing parent, or seeing that a disabled child is able to get to the right summer camp.

One of the hallmarks of social work competency is the ability of workers to establish effective interpersonal relationships with clients. This requires the worker to attempt to enter the world of the client psychologically, to create enough of a sense of empathy and establish sufficient rapport to elicit a description of the problem as seen by the client. In other words, the worker aims to understand the client's subjective reality, along with the client's feelings about the situation.

All of this, needless to say, is not an easy task, and certainly it can be argued that it is impossible for a social worker to ever fully understand the world of the client. This difficulty is compounded when a social worker is from a different culture, class, or gender than the client. Two black social work researchers in Nova Scotia write:

> It is obvious that many clients experience some discomfort in accepting help from a Black professional social worker. We have been questioned about our qualifications and many clients seem shocked (and sometimes a little skeptical!) to learn that we have graduate training from an accredited School of Social Work. We are also frequently asked about our place of birth. We are both Nova Scotian Blacks – from East Preston and Halifax respectively. Many whites, especially those from the lower socio-economic groups, find it difficult to believe that a Black Nova Scotian could have attained such a position. They find it equally hard to be in a position of having to receive help from one.[5]

Clients often feel ashamed or confused about their problem, whether it is alcoholism or unemployment or violence in the home. Therefore social workers consider it important to be skilled in asking the appropriate questions, observing, listening, and focusing on painful topics. In theory we try hard to be non-judgemental, to refrain from criticizing or blaming clients for their situations. All these skills and attitudes, at least on paper, are aimed at obtaining an accurate picture of client perceptions. Again, however, it is questionable whether social workers try to get accurate pictures of client perceptions. In actual practice we more likely focus primarily on our own perceptions, our own assessments, and our own definitions of problems, of what is "normal". This very process is what is in fact called "professional", and is a one-way process much of the time.

The skills of social work practice are rooted within social work values, such as the value and importance of the individual's dignity. The worker's expression of this value, in theory, helps to communicate to the client that the worker empathizes, respects, and understands the pressures on the client.

All of this is meant to ensure that the client no longer feels entirely alone with the problem. At a deeper level, the theory goes, the client will gain moral support through the social worker's capacity to express a genuine, caring attitude about what happens to her or him. It is also meant to help marshall the client's inner strengths to deal more effectively with the situation. A growing social work literature emphasizes the worker's ability to foster self-help groups and informal social networks as important sources of help to clients.

Very frequently, however, these theories and intentions break down in practice. When caseloads number well over 160 individuals and families, it becomes impossible for the worker to know clients except on a superficial level:

> From a service point of view, I don't even have time to listen to clients. In one recent month my total caseload was over 215 cases! I burnt out last August. During one hour then I had as many as five cases of evictions to deal with. It got to the point that emotionally I gave as little as I could to each client. Of course clients realize it and get resentful.

The awareness that families have immense influence on the individual has led to the practice of including family members in the helping process. At times social workers meet with the family as a group, to help the system work better, more comfortably, or alternatively to help members break away from the family as constructively as possible. In marriage counselling and mediation, for example, the worker seeks to understand each family member's version of the situation without taking sides, while at the same time encouraging each person's capacity to hear the others and to express his or her needs.

In practice, rather than objectively empathizing and refraining from judgement, social workers more likely attach "blame". Social workers and other professional helpers have not been immune from the prejudices of a society where the institution of patriarchy is deeply ingrained. As Jennifer Dale and Peggy Foster put it, "Social workers avoid facing up to the feminist insight that the family is not a private haven for women but is all too often an unsafe prison."[6] In recent years feminists have studied the concept of "maternal deprivation" and how it relates to the helping professions' bias against women:

> Out of theory, devoid of everyday practice, male theoreticians have assumed that the best mothering is individualized, private, one mother to one child. According to these theoreticians, "improper" mother-child relations result in adult social deviance. In the wake of maternal deprivation theories, therefore, mothers have been held responsible by the helping professions for conditions as diverse as mental retardation, schizophrenia, delinquency, depression, incest, violent crimes, slums and prostitution.[7]

In family work, it is often the mother who is found at fault – although this attitude can be extremely well-disguised by the professional aura and its clinical tones. In their book *Feminists and State Welfare*, Jennifer Dale and Peggy Foster describe the situation of women within the nuclear family as "the daily grind of isolated drudgery". They conclude:

> Social workers still tend to blame those women who fail to cope adequately with this role.... practising social workers still tend to see depressed women as failing to perform their natural role in the family rather than as being depressed by that very role.[8]

The various ways of working – with individuals, groups, and families – typically hold one assumption in common: "that it is not the emotions themselves that create the problems, but rather the clients' inability to be in touch with their feelings or to share them with someone important."[9] For social workers this difficulty tends to constitute the core and primary source of the problem.

At the same time social workers are taught that within the psychological realm it is not enough to merely develop empathy and caring relationships with clients. The social worker is also expected to be clear about the mandate of the social service. This means that the worker must make demands on the client, even if it is a voluntary relationship. Daphne Statham, experienced in the British social work system, writes of the social worker-client relationship: "Help is conditional. The pattern of tell-me-your-problem, or, alternatively, behave-well-and-I-will-give-you-material-help, is by no means extinct in practice."[10]

An influential U.S. social work educator, William Schwartz, called this the social worker's demand for work, in which the worker reminds the client why he / she is there, so that the professional relationship itself becomes a means of achieving the purpose of the service.[11] Otherwise, the theory goes, social workers who convey a sense of empathy and caring for the client will fail to provide clients with a sense of movement against the problem. Conversely, as Lawrence Shulman, author of *The Skills of Helping Individuals and Groups*, puts it:

> Workers who only make demands upon their clients, without the empathy and working relationship, will be experienced by clients as harsh, judgmental and unhelpful. The most effective help will be offered by workers who are able to synthesize, each in their own way, caring and demand. This is not easy to do either in the helping relationship or in life.[12]

But this approach is one-sided and presumptuous. It seems to demand work from the client but only empathy or caring from the social worker. The worker is in control, in power – leaving the relationship open to serious abuse. A better approach would surely be to acknowledge that demands for work need to come from both participants – from client as well as worker – to initiate a process of mutual demands and negotiation.

The Frustration of Social Work

The vast majority of social work textbooks spend their time elaborating on how the demands of the work and the accompanying skills of creating empathy can be applied by professionals to help their clients. These elaborations include a variety of techniques from which social workers can choose, depending on the client's problem and on the type of service being offered by the agency.

Such an approach, like the idea of "demand for work", presents social work in an idealized form and assumes that the professional's relationship with the client will be governed by an unqualified concern for the client's well-being. Unfortunately, this is often very distant from the truth.

In a majority of cases, the relationship with the client is not rooted purely in the worker's concern for the client's welfare. Far from it: Social workers have their own biases, their own concerns, their own world-views to promote. There is often a visible slippage from empathy and understanding into blaming and pushing clients in preordained directions. All too often, the demands on clients are governed instead by the needs and requirements – the mandate – of the social agency, and its policies on how clients are to be treated.

Social workers may try to temper agency practices in light of what they think a client needs or wants. But the fact remains that social workers are employees who are expected to follow the agency's rules and policies. These rules in turn often place social workers at odds with clients. Supervisors are usually nearby to remind social workers about the agency's expectations. A social worker in British Columbia described such expectations within a public assistance agency:

> As a social worker, you know it's impossible for a family to stay within the food budget. But you find your supervisor is putting pressure on you – to put pressure on the client to keep within the budget.

In this way the benign-sounding "demand for work" opens the door to demands by the state, via social workers, that clients accept, conform, and adjust to the rules. This puts a squeeze on clients. It also creates discomfort for many social workers who try to maintain a sense of personal accountability, of decency and respect for others, as distinct from the requirements of the agency. As one social worker put it:

> *The rates for welfare are so inadequate that you'll often find a mother, father, and child all living in one room in a run-down hotel; it's the only place they can afford because the rent elsewhere is too high for them. The place has no cooking facilities, so they eat by going to a greasy restaurant and buying things at 7-11 and corner stores. You find mothers trying to toilet-train their child where there's no toilet in the room, so they have to go down the hall – to a toilet shared by several tenants.*

From a feminist perspective, Jennifer Dale and Peggy Foster see the limited aid extended by social workers as reinforcing inequalities:

> By acting as the rationers of scarce resources welfare professionals provide a useful buffer between women's demands and a State which will not meet those demands. Welfare professionals, rationing resources on a personal and individual basis, help to disguise the collective nature of women's oppression.[13]

Knowing that as a professional helper you aren't really going to be helping clients get on their feet produces a sense of demoralization – primarily among clients but also among social workers. After all their training, social workers discover that while their agencies do provide some help to clients, at best they can barely scratch the surface of the problem. Within agencies, tensions can build and explode. A social worker in Vancouver told me this story:

> *This rather large fellow comes up to the receptionist. You can see he's not drunk – he's stoned. He's about six-foot-five, I mean, he's big! And he asks for something. He's told by the receptionist he can get it from his own welfare office. He asks for some coins for the bus. The receptionist, an 18-year-old woman, starts to look in her purse to give him some change.*
>
> *I was in the middle of a conversation with another social worker who overhears the client asking for change. She stops talking with me, turns around and tells the receptionist, "No! Don't give it to him!" Well, that big fellow – he just blew! He swung both arms across the reception desk – the typewriters, phone, papers all went flying all over the place.*

As if this isn't enough, this social worker now tells him that I walk that distance once each day! I felt this was all crazy, that the social worker should have just shut up. I was looking around the waiting room to see if anyone else was looking to join a fight. You can get a few clients all getting angry and you can get into some pretty heavy duty stuff! Luckily everybody was still calm.

I wanted to defuse the situation fast. So I tried to change the tone by saying, "Actually, I don't walk once, I do it twice." This fellow did see the humour of it, but added his own by hissing at me – "Thhhaatssss your tough luck!!!" Meanwhile somebody had called the police. He turns to leave but before going, he points his finger at the social worker and says, "YOU'RE FUCKIN' DEAD!!!" She wilts. He walks out.

It is not only in the government sector that social agencies appear to be just scratching the surface of the problems they face. For example, a social worker employed by a community centre in the voluntary sector reflected on her services to the elderly:

We're very busy with follow-ups from referrals from hospitals and a variety of services. We can barely keep up. We don't have enough staff to do justice to the older population. We've been here for ten years, but we don't advertise our services. What would be the point? We're stretched to the limit as it is.

Similarly, an executive director of an employment project meant to aid prisoners from federal penitentiaries found herself working on a shoestring budget that had recently been cut back:

If a prisoner isn't able to find a job after release from prison, what happens? He can go on welfare but many are too proud, so where can they get money to pay for food and rent? Crime becomes very tempting and the next thing you know, they're back in prison. Our society spends a lot on punishment, jails and the like but little on positive help.

Even when there is positive help, all too often workers witness their work being undone. A social worker in the Maritimes, for instance, had developed a program for school drop-outs who were in conflict with their families and with the law. The program consisted of developing positive relationships with the youths and taking them out to work on fishing boats:

After a couple of weeks the kid would return home and the mother would tell me – "My son looks great! I don't recognize him! He's got a tan, developed a bit of muscle, the lines under his eyes are gone, the tension is gone, he looks great!"

But it was all a mirage. Those changes meant nothing ... nothing! Because these kids went right back into their old situations, there were no other choices. We had a temporary program and when it was gone, the kids were left with nothing, no jobs, just like before.

With women or girl clients there is a subtle shift in the social worker's definition of the problem: much less emphasis on unemployment, jobs, money – an explanation most often used in the case of men or boys – and far more emphasis on emotional and psychological weakness. Lawrence Shulman's textbook, for example, points out how to help a mother who has beaten her child:

The way to begin to help this mother is to break the vicious cycle where her own guilt leads to feelings of helplessness and hopelessness which in turn leads to poor parenting, which in turn ... and so on. The ability to articulate and face her feelings, sharing them with a caring and yet demanding worker, can be a beginning. The worker's acceptance of the client, including her feelings, can be the starting point for the client's acceptance of herself.[14]

In this case there is no mention of lack of resources. There are no questions asked about "Where is the father?", shared parenting, whether the father has abandoned the family, or if community services – financial and otherwise – are readily available to the single mother. Above all, there are no questions asked about whether this woman has an inalienable right to her own separate, adult existence, and whether her life situation mirrors the desperation of any and all oppressed women.

Cutbacks and Caseloads: The Professional Bind

No matter how appropriate the social workers' "demands" on their clients, no matter how sensitive their communication skills, the core of the problem seems to remain beyond their reach as professionals. Realizing that social agencies should develop better ways of working with clients, some social workers cope by trying to cut through the red tape. Usually, it's an uphill struggle. As a parole officer working with offenders inside federal prisons said:

> When you visit the pens as a parole officer to plan for conditional releases, you discover more injustices. You try and do something about it but others in the bureaucracy are afraid. So people do their jobs and the bureaucrats can always say "Sorry, but that's the rule."

As a consequence, social workers experience a sense not only of powerlessness – at least with respect to management and control of the work – but also of futility as they experience the inertia of their institutions. Of course, this may not be the case with all social agencies. But it is the case very frequently and holds true for most client populations regardless of province or region. An apt description focuses on social workers' morale in Ontario child welfare agencies:

> Inundated with paperwork, constantly under stress, unsure of policy or direction, they are more concerned with keeping the lid on than exposing the garbage. And with budget cuts and growing caseloads, morale is bad. There is a feeling that no one gives a damn, and even if they do, they can't do anything about it.[15]

As a result, while it is possible that social services to individuals, families, and groups may be offered in a useful and humanitarian manner, social workers find their competency undermined by the very context in which they work. Is it any wonder that some professionals drop out? It begins with a yearning to escape, as one social worker told me:

> The other day I heard about someone on the west coast, he built himself a small house on top of a tree, overlooking the ocean. I really like that idea, imagine letting the wind come and swaying you in that tree and just being free. I might go and find a tree like that....

Most of us, however, have been trained to hang in, for various reasons. If we can just persist a bit longer and do the best we can, there may be a promotion not too far down the road. Or things might get better. We might tell ourselves that as supervisors we will do more to change things. The job does have its satisfactions, after all, and sometimes these satisfactions work to prevent us from grasping the total picture.

Typically, however, the satisfactions are outweighed by the stress generated by overwork:

During the time I'm supposed to write up my clients' files, my day is interrupted by walk-ins – homeless families with nowhere to go, crises of all sorts, phone calls from anxious clients I haven't had time to call for two or three months. There've been some days I haven't gotten near my files. So I have to do it on my own time. It's difficult, some husbands get angry when you bring work home. But if you don't your supervisor is on your case. The clients are angry too because they haven't received their cheques because you haven't had time to write up their file.

We're talking basics here. It could be a family that's been evicted with five or six children; there's no groceries so they're hostile. That's why our casework is critical to their well-being. Yet the demands go beyond our energy or time. Talk of pressure! I'm developing allergies and my doctor tells me it's stress-related. Other social workers have migraines. There's been three marriage breakdowns among my co-workers. I've seen social workers becoming hysterical, breaking down and crying at the office.

Another source of conflict is the difference of opinion held by social agency managers and supervisors about the reasons for the front-liner's stress. For instance, when I was working in Alberta, seasoned social workers there were carrying what they found to be excessive workloads and had to use overtime to complete the work. The provincial department they worked for decided arbitrarily to cut back on their overtime allowances – but not on their caseloads. The explanation given to these social workers was clear: The department's budget had to be cut back; therefore do the work within regular working hours; if you can't we will have to conclude you are incompetent.

In other words, the social agency's managers had decided that the way to deal with the situation was to force the social worker into a classic speed-up, akin to the assembly line. Those workers who couldn't or wouldn't conform were deemed inefficient. This would in turn be reflected in the social worker's annual evaluation and annual salary increments. Demoralized staff would be expected to resign but there would be plenty of eager young graduates to take their places. The quality of the work seemed irrelevant, as long as the department could show good statistics for the quantity of work done. In fact, a small amount of overtime was the reward granted to the few social workers who could actually manage their caseloads under the new system.

Again, it is not incidental in cases like this that most front-line workers are women and most senior managers are male – replicating the traditional male-female positions in society.

Such tactics by management have left front-line social workers feeling vulnerable. Neither the social work professional associations nor the labour unions' negotiations with management have been able to counteract such forms of intimidation effectively.

Another social worker in Alberta recalled what happened when she had some questions about a client in a difficult situation. She went to her supervisor for some advice. She told me that what happened to her had also happened to other workers:

> Now the supervisor turns on me and says – what's the matter with you? Don't you know what to do?
>
> The thing is, the supervisor sometimes doesn't have the answer either. But instead of admitting it, the supervisor scares away the worker. After being treated that way, the worker learns not to ask again. Especially since it's the supervisor who evaluates the performance of the front-line worker.

Again, not all supervisory relations with front-line staff are like this. But such incidents happen too often to be simply dismissed as exceptions to the rule. No wonder some social workers become bitter:

> It's rather irksome when social workers are criticized, say by people outside the department, and yet management never tries to defend the quality of commitment by social workers. Meanwhile, we're sweating it out....

5

Managing Social Work: From Top to Bottom

The organization chart of a social agency shows the positions occupied by employees, illustrates the hierarchy of power, and clarifies proper channels of communication.

Canadian Social Welfare, a textbook

AS AN ACTING director of a social development agency in Montreal in the early 1970s, I was concerned about the inadequacies I saw in welfare services. When I let it be known to my co-workers and superiors that I intended to speak out on these problems, to go on public record, I received quiet yet clear messages about my "short-sightedness". Furthermore, when I joined welfare clients who were staging a sit-in at a welfare office to protest low welfare rates, many members of the agency's board saw my attitude as "unbecoming of a professional".

After that, had I wanted, for instance, to become executive director of the agency, there would probably have been sufficient opposition from the board to block the appointment. Most of the board members came from the upper echelons of society, from high positions in business and the professions. They believed in general that things were being taken care of efficiently and properly, to the basic good of all concerned. The few problems they saw were limited to "abuses" of the system, usually emanating from the client end of things. Or they saw problems as caused by "bad apples" or malcontents: social workers who were not trying hard enough to make things work; or clients who were not trying hard enough to pull themselves up by their bootstraps. At the most the problems needed some careful, judicious, and "realistic" mediating.

Such board attitudes, unfortunately, are typical of established social agencies. This is as true today as it was in the past. Elspeth Latimer, a noted scholar of social work history, observes, "Throughout the profession's history, with very few exceptions, social workers have functioned as employees of social welfare agencies under the management of lay boards," an arrangement that "simply rules out social reform activity as an integral part of the regular employment of the social worker".[1]

The reason that reform is ruled out by lay boards is that they are personally and professionally divorced from the problems that social work sets out to address. These boards see the issues from the perspective of a male dominant class that at best patronizes the predominantly female client class, at worst works to protect its own interests and to prevent any inkling of significant change. The top-down flow of power – via gender, cultural prejudices, and hierarchy – has a major impact on the maintenance of inequalities inside the social work profession.

But the hierarchical structure is not the only problem in the management of social agencies. Personally, in my own career as a rising young social worker I had other things on my side: I'm white, I'm a man, and I was educated in the middle class. Those factors are crucial in achieving a level of success in the profession of social work, as they are in most other professions.

The Stratification of Social Work

Social agencies are stratified in ways similar to most of our government and business bureaucracies. Among the reasons given for such a stratification are greater efficiency and accountability of the organization – a rationale widely accepted by the public, including the professionals within our social services. We also assume that those at the peak of the social agency's pyramid are the most qualified and competent. According to this theory it becomes a measure of one's social work abilities to be able to rise up the career ladder.

Social workers have been taught that the current structures of authority are necessary and desirable, with little consideration of whether alternative organizational structures might better serve clients. A textbook states:

> An authority structure is needed to allocate responsibility and coordinate tasks. It provides a chain of command through which decisions are made about what is to be done, who is to do it, and how and when it is to be done. Authority is vested in stratified positions and legitimized through the dispensing of rewards and sanctions.[2]

Such hierarchies are offered as "natural" and the descriptions of them tend to downplay the aspect of social control embedded in the structure. While these hierarchies offer rewards for what is considered professional competency and while they expedite the work in certain ways, at the same time they reproduce societal power relations that maintain the haves and have-nots, the dominants and subordinates, in an unequal society.

Over-work, speed-ups, cutbacks, and their effects on clients are therefore not the only reasons for demoralization among social workers. Front-line workers also experience a sense of powerlessness and frustration because of their subordination to directives issued from above. The top-down flow of power becomes, among other things, a channel for punitive actions against social workers, leading to a profound sense of alienation.

For example, in Alberta in 1981, a scathing series of "investigative" newspaper stories reported on the abuse of foster children by foster parents. The province's ombudsman conducted an investigation and reported on a case in which "The child was wrapped in bandages and trembling like a bird. He had many blisters [from burns], some very large, and bruises all over his body."[3] There were reports of children killed in foster homes.

Not long after the stories appeared, the provincial minister announced a new policy. Henceforth social workers employed by the provincial government's child protection division were to visit each foster child and each family on their caseloads once a month. As one social worker said, at first glance it sounded like "a great idea, an improvement over just letting situations drift endlessly".

But, the worker added:

> Now comes the catch, with 90 or 120 children on your caseload, plus
> all the paperwork, tell me how it's possible to carry out this policy? It
> can't work! It's impossible! Now if something blows and a child is
> harmed, the managers can say, "We have a policy, why aren't the
> workers carrying it out?" A classic case of blaming the victim! You
> answer, "But there aren't enough hours in the day," and they can't
> hear that. The managers will pass down the blame to the supervisors
> – why can't you manage your units? And the supervisors will bitch
> against the line workers – why can't you manage your cases?

The usual explanation for such scapegoating is that those who
created the policy were out of touch with the realities of the front
line. Or that the minister was not a social worker so he really did
not understand what's involved in providing social services. Or
again, since cabinet ministers are political appointees, they really
don't care about client well-being, but are instead preoccupied with
looking good so they can advance their careers and win re-election.

While there are grains of truth in all these explanations, they also
deflect attention away from the critical structural questions and
encourage us to remain focused on the competence of particular
individuals as primary causes. For social workers this focus has a
tendency to fuel our own career ambitions. We tell ourselves – if we
are men, that is – that one day we'll become senior administrators
and when we get to exercise power it won't be so arbitrary. Meanwhile, we'd better cope as best we can and co-operate with the
powers-that-be.

At the same time, entry into various levels of the hierarchy, and
promotion through it, are controlled by other systemic forms of discrimination. If you are a woman you are most likely fated to remain
at the bottom of the social work ladder, as a front-line worker. Your
bosses, however, will probably be men. If you are one of Canada's
Native people, you are much more likely to be a client than a
worker. But if as a Native person you do want to be a social worker
– and manage despite all odds to become one – you too will likely
find yourself relegated to the bottom of the agency structure.

If the constant demand for conformity doesn't wear us down and
if we retain our abhorrence of arbitrary power, promotions create
other hazards. We become divorced from front-line colleagues and
client realities. Even if we remain part of the union, as supervisors

we begin representing management. A level of mistrust towards us develops among front-line workers and we react to that mistrust. According to a supervisor in a welfare office:

> *You find you now have two levels, your previous colleagues who are still line workers and your new colleagues who are also supervisors. You find yourself talking to other supervisors about "they" at the line level, as if somehow "they" were not quite as wise as you supervisors. "They don't know".*

Gradually the separation becomes solidified. As you attend certain meetings, you have access to information and decisions that the line staff does not have. Misunderstandings can easily develop, with line staff suspecting or knowing that you are holding back information. Many supervisors do try to be open with front-line workers, and some succeed. But such openness occurs despite the agency hierarchy, not because of it.

Harassed by overwork and feeling isolated from each other, several social workers in one child welfare agency decided to improve the situation. When phone calls to the office reported potential child abuse, these workers decided to make home visits in pairs instead of alone. All the work still got done. The team approach proved to be rewarding for the workers and created a fresh level of energy and responsiveness in relation to clients. Work pressures became more manageable and morale improved. But one of the participating social workers got a severe reprimand from her male supervisor:

> *At first I thought he was joking. He went on to say that he was supposed to be in charge of the unit and that I had too much control. After I left his office I was ready to quit. It was horrible because I doubted my own capabilities and he had convinced me at least for the moment that I was in the wrong place. He never directly mentioned the changes in our unit working together and it was only later I realized that was what bothered him. He could be supportive as long as he felt he was in charge. When we took the initiative and tried to improve how we worked, he panicked, he felt he was losing control.*

Such incidents might be explained away as mere reflections of insecure supervisors, but such a rationale avoids looking at the part played by the agency structures themselves. In fact, the problem is very much part of a larger pattern. Conflict between different levels of the organization exists all the way up to the senior managers, who in turn are subordinate to top authorities. Managers are sometimes social workers, but in the public sector they often come to their positions from other fields or disciplines, such as public administration or business management. For social work managers, conflict stems not only from their efforts to protect budgets but also from priorities established higher up.

This tendency was illustrated for me by an attempt to reorganize the Federal Correction Services in Ottawa. The goal was to better integrate parole services with correctional services. However, according to one social work manager, integration made work much more difficult because it brought the parole officers into an organization primarily concerned with "security":

> Most of the administration in Ottawa is preoccupied with security, with pens and with cutting down on escapes and on hostage incidents. The whole idea behind parole is very different, we try to help the ex-prisoner make it back into the community. As it is now, there's no distinction made between our goals and the goals of the prison.

The social worker pointed out that it is not only the goals of the work that are in conflict, but also ways of implementing them:

> Let's face it. Social workers are not "paper-oriented", we have a different approach from a bureaucrat who wants us to fill out forms, statistics and reports. The main approach now in correctional services is "what's the cost?", instead of "how well are you helping prisoners?" In Ottawa they can tell you how much it costs per square foot of prisons, but what difference does that make when it comes to helping prisoners after release?

While the cross-currents of differing approaches must be navigated by social service managers, there's not much doubt about whose interests ultimately prevail. While managers may privately disagree with goals or ways of implementing them, their actions on the job usually reflect what is expected of them by top management as incumbents of these positions.

Therefore the quality of social work provided partly depends on the interests and priorities of the political party in power in any given province or at the federal level. In an age of cutbacks, social work managers feel the squeeze: Deliver social services to more people but do so with fewer resources.

Despite some discomfort, it's surprising how many social work managers are able to rationalize these demands by telling themselves that, after all, in a democracy they must be accountable to what the public wants. In this way, many senior social workers become apologists for the system. One experienced social worker, a woman who had succeeded in becoming a manager, said she had seen this happen with many of her colleagues, especially after they had assumed positions of authority within a welfare organization:

> They seem unable to separate themselves from their employer and they find themselves jumping to the defence of the system. I believe this happens when social workers become senior bureaucrats and they really want to keep their authority.

So, for workers scaling the professional ladder, what may have begun as a career with the goal of improving conditions for clients ends up by perpetuating the status quo. The reasons are clear. Higher pay, more influence, more prestige, a sense of personal security: These are considered normal goals of other occupations. Why should it be different for social work?

Similar hierarchies exist in the voluntary sector, with the main difference being that social work managers or executive directors are accountable to voluntary boards rather than to a government minister. Even this distinction is becoming blurred as voluntary agencies receive increasing proportions of their funds from governments.

Another difference is size: The voluntary agency is usually smaller than a government agency. Voluntary boards, however, are influential in giving direction to social agencies and in promoting their credibility in the eyes of major funders. As in the public sector, social work executives strive to provide their operation with effective management. This includes financial management and supervision of either departments or front-line staff, depending on the size of the agency.

While social work executives in the voluntary sector are in strategic positions to speak out about the effects of unjust social conditions upon clients, they usually don't. It's not so much that they're told to keep quiet. There's a much more subtle process at work, as administrators learn that boards prefer a smooth operation, free from community or public controversy.

Boards are usually also active in a monitoring role. As part of this role, the board has the power to hire and fire its executive director. Social work executives, therefore, realize that the board plays a crucial part not only in relation to funding bodies but also in evaluating the executive's performance. In other words, there's not only the question of the agency's financial position, there's also the matter of the executive's professional survival as manager of the agency.

Moving Up in the Profession

Agency hierarchies may reward certain competencies, but their patterns of promotions and salaries indicate that another priority is also being served, that the management of social work is governed by the larger, structural relationships of society as a whole.

In an extensive survey of nearly 2,000 workers employed in a wide range of governmental and voluntary agencies in the Atlantic region, Joan Cummings found a large over-representation of women in the lower salary categories and an under-representation of women in the higher salary ranges.[4] This pattern did not change when variables such as education and experience were held constant for men and women. Even when the type of social work tasks performed were the same, men still earned considerably more than women.

The study also compared salaries for front-line workers, or "direct practitioners", supervisors, and administrators:

> Female supervisors were paid more than female direct practitioners, but in both cases less than their male counterparts in the same category. Female administrators, on the other hand, had an average salary only marginally higher than that of supervisors and strikingly lower than their male counterparts.[5]

Cummings noted that direct practice by front-line workers was largely carried out by women, while the more financially rewarding practice of administration and supervision was largely done by men. Her evidence illustrates again a pattern that both reinforces and is reinforced by the unequal position of men and women in the larger society.

Similar findings emerged out of a task force organized by the Social Work Association in British Columbia. Investigating sexism in social work throughout that province, Mary Russell, one of the authors of the task force's report, noted:

> Of a total of fourteen regional directors for the Ministry of Human Resources in the province, twelve were male and two were female. In Vancouver, the area managers for the Community Resource Boards were almost exclusively male.[6]

In Saskatchewan, Bonnie Jeffery and Martha Wiebe found the pattern was repeated by their data: "Overall, men have and continue to earn consistently higher salaries than do women in social work."[7] In Ontario the province's Association of Professional Social Workers studied salary categories by educational level and reported, "In each educational level, women earn less than men."[8]

Given the patriarchal structure of our society, such an outcome is not surprising, even when it applies to social work, long considered a female profession. The fact that the most basic caring and nurturing of others has been systematically defined as women's work – whether paid or unpaid, whether in the home, community, or workplace – has meant that male social workers benefit by being favoured for managerial positions. While discrimination against women managers is currently being questioned via the women's movement, the question remains as to whether the minimal numbers of women in managerial positions are required to assume authority according to entrenched male patterns of domination.

Racism: The Case of Native People

As with the subordinate position of women, non-white social workers' on-the-job relationships are influenced not only by competencies and personalities but also, and more importantly, by the dominant (white male) society's relations with visible minorities. Two black women social workers in Nova Scotia have outlined some of the obstacles they face in their work:

> We have had to establish our credibility with co-workers as a prelude to building good working relationships based on mutual respect. Several of our peers are uncomfortable discussing racial issues although

they must work with Blacks and other minority groups from time to time. We have both had the experience of hearing co-workers or supervisors discuss minority groups (other than Blacks) in a negative manner. Our suspicions are that similar attitudes toward Blacks may be expressed at other times.[9]

Canadian history has abundant examples of the devaluation of different cultural groups: the missionary attitude towards the "red savages", the exploitation of Chinese railway workers, the treatment of Japanese Canadians during the Second World War, and the denial of immigration to Jews seeking refuge from Nazi regimes, to name a few.

Native people have experienced particularly harsh treatment by the economic, political, and cultural institutions of our society. The high rates of unemployment, poverty, and suicide among Native peoples are well documented.[10] These "social problems" have been largely caused and aggravated by public policies that have run rough-shod over Native cultural values and traditions. The welfare state has aimed, it seems, at converting Native people into whites. This assimilationist approach, historically spearheaded by the federal Indian Affairs department, has carried a clear message: Native cultural values are inferior to the values of the dominant society.

In a number of provinces a high proportion of social work clients, especially in areas such as child welfare, come from Native and indigenous communities. Once again, a high proportion of these clients are women.

In the late 1970s in Manitoba 60 per cent of the total number of children under the custody of social workers were Native.[11] Most of the Native children had been removed from their homes and cultures. To make things worse, a high proportion of foster parents of Native children were non-Native; the rate for Saskatchewan in 1981 was as high as 91 per cent.[12] As a result many of these children, during adolescence especially, experienced terribly confused and conflicting feelings about their personal and cultural identity.

The interests of the welfare state and Native peoples have clashed at many levels. For instance, in Calgary, Indians seeking help were turned down by officials at the provincial social services, who said they had no jurisdiction because Indians "belonged" to the federal government. Meanwhile the federal authorities six blocks away said, "Sorry, you're now off the reserve, so your problems belong to the province." Disgusted with the situation, a number of urban Treaty Indians in Calgary documented an extensive pattern of racial prejudice by white personnel in the Indian Affairs department, and ended up by occupying the Indian Affairs office in the city.[13]

There are people from Native communities who also hold social work jobs – usually the lowest paying and least secure jobs – but advancement into senior positions proves to be difficult. In fact, it is difficult for them to get into these jobs in the first place, just as it is difficult for them to enter and complete a social work education.

It was my experience as a university teacher of social work that Native students would tend to drop out a few weeks after beginning their courses. It was not for lack of trying, or intelligence, or desire. It was more a matter of culture shock: Coming out of communal traditions, living and going to school on reserves where one family often shared a small house, Native students found university to be an alien experience. They found long hours of individual study, a series of different courses, each with different students, sharp competition for grades, heavy demands from strange professors. For many it proved more than they were able to cope with.

Despite good intentions, schools of social work have generally lacked an appreciation of the impact of racism on clients, social workers, and communities. The focus of social work education on the "individual case" presents a contrast to indigenous patterns that emphasize the roles of extended families, elders, and the surrounding community. It has also been my experience that university teachers who take a sensitive and diligent approach to the needs and interests of Native students – indeed, to any students – are not especially valued. What counts for Deans who want to put their schools on the map is not the quality of relations between teachers and students. What is more likely to count is: How many research grants have you obtained lately? How many scholarly articles or books have you published?

A major hurdle for Native students is facing the accusation from family and friends that they're abandoning their people to join the "white man's" world. The bitterness of this accusation becomes more understandable when you consider the historical and current grievances of Natives against white society. Whether it is the hidden or blatant prejudices of white townspeople or urban employers, or whether it is the trivialization of Native culture by Hollywood movies and TV programs, the institutions of the dominant society have left little room or respect for the expression of authentic Native values. When Native students find themselves confronting these realities through their social work training, they face another painful question: Should they continue to train in a field which is responsible for such attacks on their culture? Will they inevitably be collaborating with a white welfare state that is perpetuating a colonial relationship with their people?

Despite these poignant questions, some Native students find they have an overwhelming desire to do social work. They feel that despite the damage inflicted on their own people by the social service delivery system, surely they can contribute something worthwhile – and, indeed, who better than they?

Of those who graduate, however, some become disillusioned as they find themselves accepted neither by white society nor by their own community. A small number of Native professionals seem to have succeeded in bridging the two cultures. Those Native social workers who aspire to managerial positions find that they can gradually receive promotions. But because the social services have not been exempt from racism, these workers also find that their upward mobility tends to be slower than whites and very few are allowed to reach the most senior posts. Meanwhile, if they have retained their credibility in their Native communities, the personal and political tensions remain, because the questions that face all social workers can become brutally stinging when one Native person asks another: Whom are you working for? Our people? The white man's agency? Or just for yourself?

The Roles and Goals of Management Techniques

Not surprisingly, social work managers have tended to borrow their business philosophies and techniques from the corporate world. These techniques, along with their computer-aids, are presented as scientific and as a means of promoting more effective delivery of social services. There are also strong claims that such approaches can improve staff morale. Those who are suspicious of these new techniques find themselves on the defensive. After all, how can anyone be against scientific progress, against more effective services, or against better staff morale?

An example of a management technique borrowed from business and applied to social work is MBO: Management By Objectives. This procedure held out the promise of improving the quality of social services and of improving employee morale. The Canadian Association of Social Workers sponsored a project to apply MBO to four social agencies located across the country.[14]

Peter McMahon, who headed this project, helped these social agencies apply MBO in their services. He relied on previous research that had analysed social service jobs and had boiled them down to 367 specific job tasks.[15] Focusing on these specifics, McMahon encouraged management and employees to practise "participatory management", that is, participation by all parties in hammering out an agreement about who should do which tasks in the social agency. The hope was to blend the employees' needs and objectives with those of the organization.

McMahon's enthusiasm for MBO was based on the element of participation as well as upon the expected outcome of such participation: better assessment of work performance leading to better social services. But not everyone shared his optimism. Neil Tudiver, University of Manitoba, pointed out that "Methods of the detailed division of work and its careful monitoring and control, have been applied to the work of many social workers". Tudiver argued that these forms of management came from "production settings fundamentally different from the production and consumption of social services", and concluded: "These systems are inappropriate and thus potentially misdirected, useless and harmful."[16]

One of Tudiver's concerns was that the act of splitting social work tasks into small bits and pieces would separate the "thinking parts" of the job from the "doing parts". Further, by skimming off the "thinking parts" from front-line workers, the result would be an intensified form of control exercised by social service managers. Tudiver warned that such developments would further reduce the range of judgement exercised by front-line workers. He concluded that even though MBO emphasizes the sharing of management-employee objectives, this merely masks the interests of management in exercising complete control over the work process. In fact, the problem is that such "sharing" can only happen between equal partners. The "objectives" ignore the established power relations.

McMahon admits that with MBO, management can impose its

objectives on its staff. Such imposition, he feels, would be a mistake and he therefore urges managers to refrain from it. If managers were willing to accept this advice, it might seem reasonable for front-line workers to welcome MBO. Besieged by crisis, frustration, and a sense of powerlessness, front-line workers would notice a definite change if management suddenly offered to listen and to give them a voice or a significant role in decision-making and setting goals. But again, like all voluntary programs – such as affirmative action for women and people of colour – power remains in the same hands, and the rhetoric masks the reality.

Employee participation in goal-setting, McMahon points out, can easily slip into greater participation than originally expected. In other words, participation could be less welcome if it starts to have real impact. In McMahon's words the situation could be "potentially dangerous if an issue under discussion has policy implications and appropriately belongs to senior management".[17] One wonders, "dangerous" for whom? For management? For workers? For clients? McMahon implies that only management can decide whether policy implications "appropriately" belong to senior management. He seems to be saying that participation by front-line staff is desirable only insofar as it doesn't threaten the prevailing hierarchies.

Upon closer analysis, it is clear that such business techniques have not delivered on their promise of providing more effective services. What they have succeeded in doing, however, is to further entrench power within management, leaving social work staff even more dependent upon directives from above.

In class terms, just as the interests of managers in private enterprise become identified with the owners, managers of social agencies (and most of their consultants) identify primarily with the interests of those in control of the social service delivery system. In both cases, front-line employees emerge as a separate group, subordinate and subservient to the power of the managerial group. Managerial techniques, then, by intensifying this division, ultimately serve to further alienate the relatively powerless front-line workers.

Such techniques are also making it possible for social agencies in the public sector to accelerate the trend to more centralized agency control. This trend has been documented by a study of Quebec's network of community centres (CLSCs), established in the early 1970s to provide a range of health and social services.[18]

In the first two years of operation, social workers were activating community groups who were having a say in the direction of these centres. The Quebec Ministry of Social Affairs, however, then decided to streamline, standardize, and centralize these centres. As a result, the community groups soon became rubber stamps, with decisions made by senior management in Quebec City. When the centre directors, who were also managers, decided to resist this centralization, they explicitly gave moral support to staff and to associated community groups, all of whom acknowledged the value of autonomy for the centres. At about this time, professional front-line workers used their union to press for better working conditions. The Ministry "reminded" the centre directors that the directors were essentially employers and therefore had to oppose the union's position. The Ministry's views prevailed and the directors lined up (though in some cases reluctantly) behind the Ministry's position.

This illustration points to the enormous leverage exercised by senior social service managers. In addition, a McGill University study looked at workers' grievances under collective agreements with the Quebec Ministry of Social Affairs. This study found that decisions by labour arbitrators tended to bypass "professional" considerations – such as the priority of a client's well-being – itemized by the social work code of ethics.[19] Instead, arbitration proceedings emphasized the principles of employer-employee relations, as practised within the world of business corporations. As a result, Quebec arbitration proceedings upheld management prerogatives in the assignment and definition of work tasks. According to these management prerogatives, loyalty and obedience to the organization is expected from all employees, including social workers. Most of these social workers are women, who in many key areas of their lives – family, paid workplace, church, and school – have been required to submit to male authority. As workers they are often torn apart by a mixed sense of loyalty and commitment – to the agency (and therefore to the managers), to the clients, to themselves. Blaming the client, the "victim", is often the outcome of such powerlessness.

Client interests and needs thus become defined entirely by the employer. While this has the effect of shrinking the scope of professional autonomy by front-line workers, the thrust of these arbitration decisions is congruent with the social relations within private corporations. Those, after all, are rooted in the judicial doctrines of the master-servant relationship.

Given this leverage by social agency managers, it appears that social work is being granted professional status only in a symbolic sense. Although its professional associations can discipline their own members for unethical conduct, social work associations have no clout when it comes to protecting a practitioner from authoritarian directives issued by social agencies. The real control over practice is not exercised by the profession but rather by a smaller group of agency and welfare state managers.

The Push to Private Practice

Class relations within social work organizations are not confined, however, to the typical social agency. Private practice has its own link to class structure. Ironically, one reason for the growth of private practice was the disenchantment by professionals at the social control over their practice by agency managers.

This resulted in some social workers deciding to manage their own social services by setting up private offices, much like dentists or lawyers, and charging fees for their services. Sometimes several social workers have joined together in partnerships or other arrangements, or have formed consulting firms seeking contracts – for example, to carry out staff development programs for established social agencies. These private social work businesses are not viewed as "social agencies" because that term normally refers to a non-profit approach to social work.

Social workers who have opted for private practice do succeed in escaping the regulations and policies of social agencies. One private practitioner expressed relief at no longer having to work for what he saw as a government monopoly over social services. Yet, although these social workers are no longer constrained by bureaucratic rules, they create a different kind of constraint by bringing the principles – and necessities – of capitalism directly into their delivery of services.

In order to generate profits, these workers must charge a fee for their service. Who will be able to pay? Almost always, it is a middle-class clientele. In exchange for payment, such clients receive counselling on how to better cope with family tensions, work pressures, and personal troubles.

Private practitioners also obtain lucrative work from government agencies that contract out, for example, family assessments to be used in juvenile court. When social workers carry out such contracts for a state agency, they come back full circle in collaborating with the welfare state. True, they have won a measure of independence in their day-to-day work; they are no longer civil servants. But when they receive government contracts, they are expected to carry out work which does not question the institutional arrangements of power.

Moreover, while exceptions exist, most social workers in private practice become more and more profit-oriented. This promotes not only certain attitudes, but also certain forms of relationships with clients and government that parallel those inherent in business enterprises. Furthermore, if these private practitioners find they can manage their businesses and make a living at it, the lesson is that capitalism does work – it has for them. In this way, they not only affirm conservative ideology but also act in ways that perpetuate its structures.

Despite some controversy over private practice, social workers who have opened private offices have been accepted by professional social work organizations. Such acceptance among social work's official organizations has paved the way for a much larger expansion of private enterprise into the social services. There is a definite trend, much of it imported from the United States, of having private corporations organize large-scale services in day care, hospitals, nursing homes, children's group homes, and other social services. These private chains may charge their customers directly or receive a flat rate from the government, getting, for example, so many dollars per bed.

Since the primary objective is to maximize profits, their emphasis is on a mass service with a strong incentive to cut costs. Ernie Lightman states, "There is a growing array of data to suggest that higher profits are most likely to be achieved through the lowering of service delivery standards."[20] Despite telling evidence that private nursing homes have frequently failed to provide humane patient care, even periodic public scandals have failed to stem the tide of providing essential social services on the basis of private profit. Any semblance of public discussion about social needs, about how best to deliver quality service, and about prevention, is then reduced to financial decisions by shareholders within these private companies.

Another feature of this development of social work for profit is the emergence of a hierarchy of service from deluxe to inadequate.

Of course, services then become equated with hefty price differentials. All this is rationalized as getting what you pay for. Just as you have choices in buying cars, why shouldn't you also have choices in purchasing social services? In a twist of irony, the very social services which were supposed to modify the inequalities produced by the system in the first place end up by being sold to those most able to afford them.

This begins looking like medical services in the United States – just another commodity with quality depending on your ability to pay. It is noteworthy that the U.S. medical profession not only fails to see this as a problem, but has also been at the forefront of blocking reform.

When a model such as "fees for service" is being adopted, it makes one wonder about the implications for social services in Canada. Is it too far-fetched to predict that as social work attempts to expand its professional credibility, it will gradually embrace the corporate model and turn its back against the have-nots?

To succeed in such a scenario, the profession would have to cover up its behaviour by carefully conveying a double message. By issuing periodic public statements, social work professional associations would declare their commitment to social justice, to helping the poor, the powerless, and the unemployed. Meanwhile social work would also earn a reputation among decision-makers for having tough-minded managers capable of keeping their staff in line and their clients in their place. If social work managers were able to convince line professionals that the best way to be helpful to clients is by accepting the agency's constraints, the next step would be for front-line workers to pass this message on to their clients. From the vantage point of many clients, that future is already here.

6

Unemployment to Welfare to Poverty: Clients Speak Out

I have $11 a month to buy food after I pay my rent.... Last night I had to run around the street looking for a blanket because it was so cold. I just want to tell people I am so hurt. I am so depressed.

> a twenty-year-old woman on welfare, speaking to Canada's first national conference on hunger, November 1986

THE ECONOMIC CONDITIONS of the 1980s have amplified the need for the services of the social work profession. They have also highlighted the underlying structural causes of social distress: The invisible walls are becoming more and more discernible. The 1980s started with an official unemployment rate of over 10 per cent and despite fluctuations the rate remains higher than at any period since the depression of the 1930s.

But these figures represent only the official version. When you add people who are working part-time, often because they can't find decent full-time jobs, plus those who have given up looking altogether because there are not enough jobs to go around, the actual unemployment rate nationally becomes something like 15 per cent.[1]

Excluded from that rate are women who are carers in the home (but might prefer to work outside the home if they could find jobs), whose work is not considered productive because they toil within the reproductive side of our economy. As Dorothy O'Connell puts it, "Raising wheat is work, driving a garbage truck is work, raising children is nothing."[2] Margrit Eichler adds:

> Until very recently most people were unaware of the fact that unpaid household work is in fact work. Why on earth is this a new insight at a theoretical level? Women have known it all along. However, if you look at economic theories and at the way, for instance, economists, sociologists or other people who write about these issues deal with them, it is a totally new and revolutionary insight.[3]

Then there are those many people who have had to accept jobs at minimum or poverty wages – simply because employers are allowed to get away with it.

The conditions also differ regionally. In Newfoundland in 1985-86 the official jobless rate was given as 20 per cent. Again, according to a research study carried out by Canada's three largest unions – the Canadian Union of Public Employees, the National Union of Provincial Employees, and the Public Service Alliance of Canada – this rate is an underestimate. The research report concludes that full-time regular employment in the province is a "minority phenomenon".[4]

High unemployment erodes the gains made by women for access to jobs and to independent incomes. Their bargaining position, being weak, makes them probable candidates to be first to lose their jobs or to settle for lower wages. Native people and immigrant non-white workers are also likely to experience limited choices and to settle for low-paying, non-union, unsteady, and unreliable jobs. Curiously, this reinforces attitudes portraying them as unsteady and untrustworthy individuals.

With limited access to decent jobs, crime can appeal as a career, which in turn closes more doors. A young black adult gave a graphic account of the impact of racism and a "clouded" personal history on job searching.

Then I went to manpower to look for jobs. I remember the place smelt like a tavern. I was given a name and a phone number, so I called and made an appointment. When I went up to the office, there were two women sitting in the waiting room. I sat down and waited too. This fella comes out of the office and calls out my name. I said "Yes, I'm here" and I stand up. The fella looks up from his file, sees my face and freezes. Why he practically pushed me down on the chair! I knew I had no chance at a job there.

And anyhow, whenever I apply for a job right on the application form there's a section that says, do you have a criminal record? When you put down "yes", that finishes your chance for a job.

High unemployment not only affects the most vulnerable in the workforce – women, non-whites, and youth – but it also undermines the labour movement's victories from an earlier era, victories that promised secure income to anyone willing to become employed. When Unemployment Insurance benefits run out, or if an applicant does not qualify, the source of support shifts away from the federal government to provincial and municipal public assistance (or welfare) programs. The Social Planning Council of Metro Toronto has documented a direct relationship between higher levels of unemployment and higher welfare caseloads.[5] Furthermore, the 1986 federal Task Force on Program Review notes that 10 per cent of Canadians are on welfare, adding, "Roughly half that number is on welfare because of the lack of employment and this is over and above the number receiving UI support."[6]

In Ontario, from 1982 to 1986 the number of women, men, and children collecting welfare payments increased by 32 per cent. In Sault Ste. Marie, an Ontario town dependent on an ailing steel industry, the number of people on welfare increased by a staggering 85 per cent in the same four-year period. That town's welfare administrator concluded that, more and more, unemployment had become invisible as thousands of people across Canada had run out of unemployment benefits or given up looking for jobs.[7] These are the "discouraged unemployed". This administrator's comments echo those of other welfare officers across the country. The general manager of Metro Toronto's social services department stated, "People just aren't finding a place in the economy."[8] This is borne out by Statistics Canada, which has documented the fact that, in contrast to those who can find other work in a few weeks, a large proportion of the unemployed are the longer-term unemployed.[9]

Social workers have known for a long time that unemployment produces enormous social and personal stress. If further evidence is needed, it is supplied by Dr. Harvey Brenner of Johns Hopkins University, who examined the effect of unemployment in the United States. He found strong correlations between a sustained rise of 1.4 per cent unemployment in the early 1970s and other increases: 5.7 per cent more suicides, 4.7 per cent more state mental health hospital admissions, 5.6 per cent more state prison admissions, and 8 per cent more homicides.[10] Sharon Kirsh, editor of the Canadian Mental Health Association's report *Unemployment: Its Impact on Body and Soul,* found evidence to suggest that "Increases in the rate of unemployment are accompanied by increases in the rates of spouse abuse, rape, child abuse, children's problems in school, criminal acts and racial tensions."[11]

Meanwhile business leaders continue to lobby for their own solution. In this process, valuable work becomes more and more equated with employment within business corporations. The value of child care in or out of the home becomes further marginalized. Public services are seen as causing deficits and as being havens for incompetents. We are told not to worry and that "the answer for job creation" is to make it as easy as possible for corporations to maximize their profits, to attract new investments, to create new jobs.

The facts present a different picture. Researcher Gordon Ternowetsky, comparing the growth in corporate profits and job creation, found that profits in the banking industry had accumulated a 402 per cent increase from 1981 to 1984, while at the same time the total number of jobs in that industry increased by less than 1 per cent. In the oil industry, the four major companies had profits of over $5 billion, but there was an actual reduction in the number of jobs.[12] When Ternowetsky examined the largest companies (from all industries) operating in Canada, he found that those which had experienced successive growth in profits from 1981 to 1984 had an average profit growth of 97 per cent – while at the same time their average employment was reduced by 3 per cent.[13]

Some economists have concluded that regardless of how often the business community promises to create the necessary jobs, it won't happen. In their view high unemployment is not an interruption of economic growth, but is a direct consequence of it, due partly to the job-displacing technologies. French writer André Gorz argues:

What is happening is that industrial society is doing its best to hide
the fact that the amount of socially necessary labour is declining rap-
idly and that everyone could benefit from this. Instead of proposing
more free time for all those who want it, the only choice being offered
is between full-time work or full-time unemployment – which is a
way of presenting free time as a disaster, as social death.[14]

Gorz proposes that the benefits of technology be shared throughout
the entire population by replacing capitalism with alternative democratic and community-oriented institutions designed to strengthen
the autonomy of individuals as well as their co-operative potential.

Such an approach to sharing is a far cry from what happens
today, when the impact of advanced technology is widening the gap
between the haves and have-nots.

Given the immense hardships associated with an inadequate supply of jobs, what has the welfare state done about it? Federal government policies and programs, led by unemployment insurance,
along with job training and job creation efforts, have been revised
and reorganized. But have these programs and efforts been effective?

Social policy researcher Graham Riches pursued this question by
analysing the growth of food banks, which were virtually unknown
prior to 1980. He documents the emergence of 90 food banks
across the country. These food banks serve mainly welfare clients,
but are also used by recipients of unemployment insurance, who
find that the government cheques are too small to cover all their
basic needs. Riches points to the sharp rise in food banks as concrete evidence that "Programmes such as unemployment insurance
and provincial social assistance are failing in their official objectives
and are inadequate to the task".[15] He argues that such failure is tan-
tamount to the collapse of the social security safety net. The collapse, he says, is consistent with the fact that government policy and
business practices are largely responsible for the growth of unemployment. Ernie Lightman, an economist at the University of
Toronto, also argues:

The unemployment which follows almost inevitably from reduced
government involvement in society has been relatively focused, concentrated mainly in certain groups who have borne the brunt of
exclusion from paid work within our society.[16]

It has become painfully clear who these certain groups are: non-whites, recent immigrants, the elderly and youth, with women cross-cutting all of these categories. If finding a decent job is next to impossible for so many people, what do they find and experience when they turn to the welfare system for help?

Entering the Welfare System

It has become commonplace for people in need to desperately try to avoid getting into the welfare system in the first place. Part of this is a matter of personal pride and hopes alongside a prevailing sense of the work ethic, a belief that the individual has to look after her or himself and not go to the state for handouts. This is a basic tenet of dominant liberal ideology – the belief that each individual has both the responsibility and the opportunity to "make it". The ideology avoids any serious consideration of community or collective responsibility for poverty and for social improvement.

This same reluctance to accept welfare is also held by non-white minorities, as one researcher found when he talked to the staff of the YMCA Youth Employment Services (YES), a community agency working in the outer-city Jane-Finch area of Metro Toronto, an area with a high-density population of visible minorities and a high level of unemployment: "The YES staff noted that welfare referrals included few blacks, possibly because West Indian immigrants don't like being called 'welfare cases', and tend to take pride in their educational and employment aspirations."[17]

When the uncertain status of being on welfare is added to the fact of colour the barriers become formidable, and not just in cases of employment:

> With six children I had a terrible time finding a place to live. When they found out I was on welfare, lots of places wouldn't rent to me. The fact I was a single parent made it worse and it didn't matter to them the fact I was widowed. Most people don't like to admit that there are people who have to live on welfare, so they push that idea aside. I've had doors slammed in my face!
>
> The fact that I'm an Indian woman makes it even worse. One place I called, the woman said "Yes, I have a place available" and so I went there. As soon as she sees I'm brown she says, "Sorry we don't rent to Native people."

There is most often a debilitating sense of dehumanization in being on welfare. Given that their child care work is constantly being devalued as non-work, a feeling of desperation often haunts women with low incomes. Dorothy O'Connell writes: "That is why some women will shoplift before they go on welfare, will bounce cheques, will almost starve themselves and their children before taking that last step."[18]

For many women, taking that last step leads to other problems:

> I did a favour to this neighbour, she was going into hospital to have a baby, so I offered to babysit her two children. Fine? Her husband comes to my place and you know what he wants? He wants to go to bed with me! I refuse and he says, "You'll be sorry." He figures I'm on welfare, I'm a single parent – I'm fair game. I told him where to go.

One woman on welfare said that it is not much different from being married – either way you get "put down all the time – that's pretty hard for the head to take!"

> My rent just went up $125. Welfare tells me to find somewhere cheaper. I tell them I've been looking and even got a letter from the housing registry that says I should stay where I am because I'm paying the going rate and there are so few vacancies in Vancouver. But welfare won't pay for the increase ... you get to feel that they're blaming me for the fact my husband took off.

Another welfare client put it this way:

> As a single parent on welfare, you feel so vulnerable, so unprotected. You're game for the wierdos on the streets. I've got a double lock on my door, but that doesn't stop the strain – the strain is financial and emotional and it can get to your health too.

When this strain is assessed by professional helpers – the social workers – it is often diagnosed, especially in the case of women, as the client's own psychological or psychiatric problems; as Helen Levine states:

> Men's stress and distress are generally linked with occupational hazards – too much pressure or responsibility on the job or unemployment – or absence of adequate nurturance and support at home. For

women, stress and distress are typically defined as mental health problems. Our turmoil is not linked to the occupational hazards of child-care and domestic labour, to poverty, unemployment or the double work-load, to the misogyny that assaults us daily at multiple levels. We are not expected even to claim a support system at home – we are supposed to provide it. Women's distress is said to be primarily "in the head".[19]

Social work counselling has equated women's unhappiness with "sickness" when the sources of that unhappiness have been the profound oppression of women in and beyond the family, in the paid and unpaid workplace. When social workers define human struggles as being mainly in the head, they help to further immobilize women, to add another load, another stigma, onto the burdens women are expected to carry.

The idea of women in social distress being somehow "sick" is connected in part to the witchcraft trials of the sixteenth century, where "witches" were often poor elderly women beggars and the accusations of witchcraft in part an attempt by rich men to get them out of the way, to avoid the guilt they might otherwise feel by seeing them huddling outside their doors every day, begging.[20] Helen Levine observes:

> Contemporary women are no longer called witches and burned as in the Middle Ages, but are instead helped to self-destruct. This self-destruct training is an insidious tool used to contain women's rage and despair, to invalidate our experience of the world. It produces guilt, anxiety and depression – a sense of impotence that keeps us docile and fearful, unable to act on our own behalf. The helping professions, in practice as in theory, collude with and reinforce the self-destruct mechanism in women.[21]

Officially, of course, social programs do not put anyone down. On the contrary, welfare programs are increasingly linked to job training programs, to affirmative action policies, and the message to clients is: We will help you re-enter the job market. And most clients welcome an improvement over inadequate welfare rates. As a result, social workers have developed job training courses aimed at improving the client's communication skills, grooming, and self-esteem, all in preparation for job interviews and for keeping jobs after being hired.

For women on welfare who are also single parents, there's a special irony to these projects; they urge women to go out and find work, as if raising children involved no work. When these women do find salaried jobs, they often are in underpaid clerical or domestic positions.[22] All this assumes that day care can be arranged (often impossible since there aren't enough day care spaces available, and the cost is financially prohibitive for many would-be users). While there's nothing wrong with the upgrading of personal skills, there's something terribly wrong with implying that such training projects are an answer to poverty and unemployment.

Social Services: A Major Disenchantment

A decade and a half ago the Special Senate Committee on Poverty provided the public with a glimpse into what it saw as a highly unsatisfactory situation. It commented critically on the approach then used by welfare offices: "It repels both the people who depend on the hand-outs and those who administer them. Alienation on the part of welfare recipients and disenchantment on the part of welfare administrators were evident in much of the testimony."[23]

More specifically for clients, the social service delivery system is a dehumanizing one, where human need is given short shrift. Clients are subtly reminded again and again that they belong to an inferior sex and / or culture, as well as an economically inferior class of citizen. One client remarked on how she felt treated inside an agency:

> The way they look at the dollars — it's like they just ring up their figures on a cash register. You're worth so much for this, so much for that — they make you feel like an animal.

Outside the agencies there are also problems:

> At a grocery store once, when I had a voucher* — it's on a piece of blue paper, they have to fill it in, then you have to sign it — I had spent

* Food vouchers are certificates that can be used in place of cash at certain grocery stores, and are sometimes granted if a family runs short before the end of the month.

fifty cents less than the amount of the voucher. One cashier shouts over to the next cashier, "Hey, here's someone with a voucher, can I give her change?" The other one answers, "No, you're not supposed to give them any money." I felt like they were talking about somebody who wasn't a person. I just wanted to tell them to forget about it, keep the damn change! Instead they were shouting and the whole store knew I was on welfare.

Such events month after month demoralize clients. Because the amount that welfare departments allow for rent is typically much lower than the actual rent charged, the recipient has to make up the difference from the food budget. In some provinces clients are allowed to receive a financial supplement to buy food, but this is only a loan. As one person on welfare said:

> They'll subtract this amount from you next cheque, so you're short next month and you always end up being short. Always behind. You get the feeling that's the way they want it.

The dynamics lead to clients feeling trapped. Even when, as happens occasionally, the rates are raised, the trap remains:

> Sometimes welfare gives us a raise — at last. We won't be eating macaroni. But nothing changes. Because then the rent goes up and wipes out the raise.

The irony here is that this woman was living in public housing: The rent was raised by the public housing authority. So what one branch of government was "giving" with one hand, another branch was taking away with another.

Continual demoralization often leads to further personal crises, shattering the welfare recipient's sense of self — what remains is a shadow of the person, which is then duly imprinted by social workers onto the official files of the state:

> Of course you never see the files that welfare keeps on you. If you're in the office and the worker gets called out, she'll take your file with her. Yet it's our life! So they have us by the strings. We're their puppets. And you better dance!

Most social workers do not consciously enjoy controlling "their" clients. Indeed, most of them would be annoyed at the suggestion that they manipulate clients to keep them in their place. There are no job descriptions calling for the manipulation of clients. The imposition of social controls is often subtle and confusing because officially clients are not presented as people to be subjugated. On the contrary, modern social work literature presents the client in a positive light:

> The client has rights – the right to service, the right to participate, the right to fail.... The client has strengths, modes of adaptation, and ways of coping. The client brings a particular set of motivations, capacities and opportunities.[24]

While this is the theory, in practice most clients find that the rights and strengths do not shine through the bureaucratic haze. Indeed, how can clients avoid feeling resentment when they come into an office and face, as one person described it, a "young twenty-two-year-old behind a desk"?

> *You can't help but wonder: What the hell does this person know about it? They may try to help, but they're so young, have so little experience, that you feel they just have no way of understanding what you're up against. Especially if they've just gone through school and just know about coping well. What do they know about not coping well?*

Perhaps the most extreme – and therefore revealing – case of alienation of client from worker comes in the restrictive institutional settings of prisons or mental hospitals. In prisons, social workers and other helping professionals, such as chaplains and psychologists, are hired as part of programs defined as "opportunities for social, emotional, physical, personal, and spiritual development". According to the Solicitor General's Office, "Each offender's program is monitored by professional staff who also counsel the offender and assess his or her program."[25] It is all in the name of "rehabilitation".

> *Rehabilitation? I get a laugh when a judge says he's giving you a jail sentence so you can get "rehabilitated". What rehabilitation? It's a*

big farce. There's only rehabilitation in the imagination of the judge.
When you get sent to prison, there's a piece of paper and it tells them
to take you from point A to point B. Point B is prison. The prison gets
the piece of paper and the only *thing they do, they try to keep you
there.*

The major irony is the belief that rehabilitation can happen at all in
a cell block or in the wards of a mental institution, where behaviour
is monitored and severely restricted and the main requirement is to
conform to behavioural norms established by administrators and
professionals.

There have been numerous accounts of women's experiences
inside psychiatric institutions. Phyllis Chesler, in *Women and Madness,* documents how most of the 24 women she interviewed had
been put into these institutions "wholly against their will, through
brutal physical force, trickery, or in a state of coma following
unsuccessful suicide attempts". This and other accounts have
depicted the institutions as more like prisons than like places
designed to help patients.[26] In another account a woman recalls the
missed opportunities for sharing concerns with other women
patients in a psychiatric institution:

> Patients said almost nothing at the ward meetings except for
> announcement of activities. And then it ended. I had been intrigued
> by the idea of this group, its possibilities. I know there have been all
> kinds of complaints and concerns and so afterwards asked G. why
> there were no comments, no grievances aired. The reply – fear,
> *FEAR,* **FEAR.** Patients are worried about the grapevine from most of
> the nurses to the doctors, their "dossier", the repercussions that
> might arise if real problems were aired. So everyone keeps mum. It's
> power politics and the women are clear re who holds the power.[27]

Is it possible to "rehabilitate" women, whether in mental hospitals
or prisons, without giving them the means – and the right – to come
together to give voice to their experience and oppression; or without giving them the means – and again, the right – to refuse the prescriptions of society and to transform their own lives? A woman
who has experienced a psychiatric institution comments:

> I know that women are drugged, in and out of hospital, to keep us

silent and subdued. I know that more and more women are resorting to alcohol and drugs in a desperation born out of coping with and adjusting to unequal, subservient everyday lives. I know the deadly guilt, anxiety, and stress that are frequently borne by women in the wife-and-mother role. I know the pretence women try desperately to maintain about the joys of motherhood, the joys of sex, the joys of nurturing others, and the joys of self-denial and service. The social control of women works well for the patriarchy.[28]

The revolving door syndrome common within prisons and mental-health services illustrates that social workers fail in their rehabilitation efforts more often than not – and it is the punitive nature of the institutions that prevails:

> *You get hardened. So if I'm walking down a cell block and someone is stabbed, I keep walking. I don't see nothin' and I don't say nothin'. You keep your mouth shut for your own good.*

Prisons and other institutions are more than locks and high walls. The pressure to adapt to the dominant view of class, gender, and ethnic background is everywhere. Invisible walls accompany our social relations whenever we interact with others. These walls stretch on throughout our lives, and the toll is high.

Workers and Clients: Constraints and Contracts

In practice, the whole business of social assistance is a matter of constraints experienced by both workers and clients. Front-line workers live with severe constraints in their paid work; the constraints of cutbacks, of mounting paperwork, growing caseloads, lack of time, and strict controls, via policies and procedures, over the exercise of judgement and compassion. The critical difference is that clients live with severe constraints in their daily, on-going lives – double constraints if, like the majority of clients, you are a woman; triple if, for instance, you are a Native woman or an Asian immigrant woman.

Within certain confines it is possible for worker and client to arrive at a mutual understanding (if that is indeed a goal) about what will be worked upon, what has priority, and how the work will proceed. Relatively speaking, however, the social worker is in a much stronger position of control and not infrequently the "contract" between worker and client is presented by the worker on a take-it-or-leave-it basis. The relationship is not one of shared power, but a one-up-one-down unequal working relationship. One person is vulnerable and in need, the other is in a position to give or withhold money, services, or advice. For a single mother, an elderly woman, or a teenage Native girl, the situation is not unlike their limited choices in employment, housing, or what food they can buy. There is little scope for bargaining over terms, especially not as individuals.

In theory, contracts between workers and clients recognize the goal of self-determination, meaning that workers are supposed to avoid imposing solutions on clients. The idea of self-determination holds that social work is effective only when clients make their own choices and decisions (with exceptions, such as when clients decide to break the law or harm others). Built upon the value of client self-determination, a social work contract is ostensibly a mutual agreement between worker and client about the goals of the service and the general method of reaching these goals. It is seen as a means of "involving" a client in making choices about what is to be done.

According to one text, the contract encourages the client "to use his or her skills and resources in the work on problem resolution".[29] A contract, then, implies equal power between social worker and client. Yet in reality there is no such equality. Most social work relationships are not one of a willing buyer and a willing seller. Most clients arrive at social agencies with little if any choice. Most often, their real choice would be not to be there at all.

All too often, social workers behave as if clients have many more choices than really exist. The workers subscribe to the myth that everyone in the society, including clients, can exercise a full range of choices on the basis of equal opportunity. Blaming the victim is the end result of such a perspective. A probation officer in the Maritimes offers one version of this approach.

> *My approach to helping inmates when they get out is clear: don't ask me to do anything more for you than you're doing yourself. I tell them you're in the driver seat and you got your foot on the pedal. Just remember I've got a foot I can put on the brake. I don't hide my authority and I'm honest about it.... You let the parolee know it's easy for you to send him back to prison. I'm trying to keep you on the*

street. They know you've got a task and sometimes it's not pleasant, but I tell them: They're the ones who decide. If they choose to do something, it's up to them. All I can do is try the best I can.

With few jobs available, with inadequate welfare payments, with the pressures of a competitive society, the relationship between client and worker reveals clearly where the social control lies. In the end it is the social worker who makes the critical decisions.

Given the stigma attached to welfare and its meagre levels of assistance, it is understandable that clients develop negative feelings about agencies and their workers. The client experience of relative powerlessness inevitably widens the gulf between client and worker. One woman, for instance, obtained a "homemaker" from the welfare office.* She commented:

> *Once I got called to the welfare office – this was after I'd had a homemaker. Welfare wanted to know – how come I didn't have enough sheets on the bed? How come there weren't enough clothes? When I came home with a few friends, I could tell the homemaker thought we were all going to be drinking. It so happens I don't drink! But they still wanted me to explain. They even asked me, how come I didn't have any coffee or tea? I was furious. I told them I go without what I like so my kids can have what they need, but I guess they couldn't understand that. Before I could even have this homemaker, they wanted to know where I was going, what I was going to do, everything. Even why couldn't I get a babysitter?*

Fear is another major factor that enters into the worker-client relationship. A client in the Maritimes said:

> *When I applied for welfare, I even knew the amount I was entitled to. It was higher than what my social worker said – but I was afraid to push for it. I was reluctant because of fear – I might lose all of it. I can now see how you become too dependent on the worker. How women's passive roles are reinforced by welfare.*

* A homemaker provides temporary service in the home, such as cooking, cleaning or child care.

Aside from the suspicion and fear experienced by clients, there is also the crippling impact of inadequate resources. The Social Planning Council of Metropolitan Toronto concludes:

> Most welfare recipients in Ontario continue to live on incomes which are 25 to 50 per cent below the poverty line. Many households on general assistance still lack sufficient incomes to cover even the basic necessities of food and shelter.[30]

Senior government officials, instead of acknowledging publicly that they represent those in power, expect social workers to accept the rationale of welfare policy, and to in turn pass on reasons like "everybody is hurting".

Broken Promises ... and Their Consequences

The net effect of the public assistance morass is to undermine the stated objectives of most welfare legislation. Provincial public assistance laws usually claim to "assist the disadvantaged" or to "provide relief to the destitute" or generally help the poor, marginal, or dislocated get back on their feet. The Canada Assistance Plan, a federal law that authorizes federal contributions to provincial welfare payments, promises to provide for "adequate assistance to persons in need and the prevention and removal of the causes of poverty".[31] Yet social workers experience these promises being broken on a daily basis by the myriad ways in which they are prevented from providing adequate help.

Clients are aware that at least some social workers find the working conditions intolerable. The good social workers either "quit or go bizarre", reported one client. The rest "become stinking bureaucrats". One person, a member of a client advocacy group, told me about getting a call from a social worker who didn't even want to give her name.

> She told me how she'd tried and tried to help a client, but she said "the system wouldn't let me". She burst out crying over the phone.

In recent years a number of provinces have amended their welfare regulations, changing the definition of who is considered "employable". In all cases the changes specified that "employable persons" would now include single parents with children of school age. In Alberta and British Columbia it was to include mothers with preschool children. Before this change, single mothers raising their children were defined as "unemployable" and therefore qualified for public assistance. The wage for their unpaid labour in the home – the "motherwork" – was low, poverty-level, but at the very least they knew a welfare cheque would arrive. They were not pressured into taking on a double workload by going out and looking for paid employment as well.

With the change of status to "employable", single mothers were now being told by social workers that they must look for paid work, or be cut off welfare. So much for freedom of choice, for recognition of the importance of children and of the hard labour that women take on in the home.

For women, the contradictions in this particular policy emerge in blatant fashion. Be a good mother, they are told, be economically self-sufficient, be superwoman. Accept a double workload, cheerfully, a load no man is expected to undertake. Our society's commitment to children turns out to be hollow, indeed, when women, as mothers, do not even have the right to their own dignified, secure adult lives, economically and otherwise.

In one province single mothers receive welfare for only four months, after which they must reapply every four months if they want to continue to get assistance. The official intention is to "help" single mothers or, in the Minister's words, to give them "encouragement to become self-sufficient through employment".[32]

This goal of pushing people towards an individual independence, towards self-reliance and away from economic dependence on a community, fits in with the general scheme of the welfare state. It also fits in with the scheme of reproducing a supply of cheap labour. But the intention is also a kind of on-going harassment of single mothers, to serve other purposes. After all, if the welfare system can be twisted into an even bigger nightmare for those on the receiving end, then even poor-paying jobs will seem attractive – shades of an earlier era. The values of the workplace, like the workhouse, are still pitted against the values of human welfare. Also out the window go the gains made by labour, and women, from the 1930s on: the minimum wage, the eight-hour day, pensions and equal pay, the right to be represented by a union. A former welfare client who is a single mother describes the consequences:

By November of last year I went off welfare. I was holding down two jobs, one with the Y, the other with a day care, but the salaries were

terribly low. I was bringing in $100 less than when I was on welfare.
So I got a third job, at another day care. All these jobs were for differ-
ent times of the day, different days of the week, but it ended up I was
working from 8:30 a.m. till 6 p.m. for five days a week, juggling these
three jobs. It was hard but I just never wanted to go back to welfare. I
felt I was better than dirt.

For the many women clients who remain trapped within poverty, the impact of welfare policies and practices makes it abundantly clear that they remain subservient to and controlled by others. In the name of public assistance women clients are systematically degraded under the guise of official policy. This remains true even though in most cases the official facing the client from across the desk or counter is another woman. Women are unfortunately and frequently divided from one another as they do the "cleaning up" of a male-defined and male-controlled society, in the home or in welfare offices.

The welfare department's authority to terminate payments creates profound fear and anxiety among male as well as female welfare clients. At first glance the policies appear to make sense. Social workers, representing the state and its proverbial taxpayers, don't want to pay out good money to people who don't need it. The department wants to know about any extra income on the part of the clients. Consequently, what usually is considered private information – gifts or inheritances or the wages of part-time employment – ceases to be private. The information becomes a matter of vital interest to the social worker, and a matter of eligibility for the recipient.

If a single mother on welfare has a male friend, does he give her any money? If so, she is expected to declare it and the amount is deducted from the next welfare cheque. Or the welfare office could decide that the woman is no longer in need of financial help and stop the cheques. Social workers and other employees of welfare offices are expected to make sure that all extra client income is declared. Again, it is a key example of a double standard of morality regarding women and men on welfare: No one asks a man who he's sleeping with. If there is a "man in the house", living with her, the rule in most provinces presumes that he must be supporting her – or he *should* be supporting her (and presumably her worries will be over).[33] There is an expectation that women exchange sexual, domestic, and child care services in return for private support.

The tension this creates for women on welfare can be intolerable. As one woman said, "I had a boyfriend and they kept asking him these questions. After a while, they just bothered him too much and he left. So they even get between you and a boyfriend."

Such client experiences give rise to the accusation of social workers being snoopy and prying into your own private business. In fact, most provinces have fraud squads as part of their welfare departments, and the job of these squads is to catch welfare applicants who say they are impoverished when in fact they are not. The most recent national survey into welfare fraud was published in *Canadian Taxation* by Reuben Hasson, a law professor at Osgoode Hall. He found that welfare claimants who are convicted of fraud constitute less than 1 per cent of all people on social assistance.[34] Yet a high proportion of clients experience harassment from the investigators. One client was still fuming at her experience:

> *This friend of mine had no job, had no place to go. I agreed to help him out. I admitted him to my place. He wasn't living with me, he wasn't giving me money. I was just trying to help him out. This causes welfare to investigate me. Now they tell me I have to report all overnight guests. Then they tell me I had to come to the welfare office. I went with an advocate from a community group. I get down there and this inspector tells us: "All people on welfare are public property!" Can you believe it!? We're now "public property"!! I got so mad!! I told him why not put me and my children in a zoo?! Can you believe it? I was lucky I had witnesses who heard him. This just gives you some idea what we have to put up with.*

In this instance the client was part of a client group whose members gave each other moral support and realized when the agency was overstepping even its normally punitive boundaries. But most clients are not so fortunate. More often than not such conduct by the agency would proceed unreported and uncontested because most clients – women especially – are verbally beaten down, socially isolated, and worn out just surviving. Clients don't necessarily see any difference between social workers and fraud investigators. Many social workers have an implicit social policing function so that in the client's eyes, workers and investigators are all lumped together as "them".

In the Interests of the Young ... and Old

The gulf between clients and social agencies is not confined to public assistance. Child welfare agencies frequently blame mothers in the name of serving and protecting children. Helping mothers establish and claim a decent life for themselves is seen to have little relation to safeguarding the "best interests of the child".

Professional theory frequently blames wife and mother in situations of sexual abuse that are typically cases of fathers abusing daughters:

> When incest occurs, professional theory and practice routinely point to the mother as having been guilty of a form of desertion within the family – having withdrawn passively or actively from vital aspects of her role, sexually and otherwise. The implication is that "normal" mothers subordinate their own needs, preferences and wishes to those of husband and children. In dealing with the sexual assault committed by husband and father, it is common practice among helping professionals to concentrate on the "inadequate" performance of wife and mother.... And if daughters were not inappropriately seductive, fathers would not "fall prey" to sexual assault.[35]

Such assumptions lead to a destructive relationship between social worker and client. An Alberta woman, for instance, became involved with social services after her husband had been found abusing her daughter:

> *Then social service made a stinking mistake. They told us my husband could come home if he took Antabuse.* Him coming back put pressure on me and pressure on my daughter, who tried suicide after that. At the time I was in stinking shape. Who knows what you're feeling when there's incest and as to social services – they knew absolutely zilch!*

Meanwhile the public gets a different version of what social workers are expected to do:

> The Department must look on each child and family as a unique situation and make available the appropriate service from a wide range

* Antabuse is a drug to curb alcoholism.

of resources.... The Department has the responsibility to provide a high quality of service to children in care, keeping in mind the child's short and long term needs in respect to *his* family, *his* community and *his* healthy functioning as a productive individual.[36]

These seemingly "lofty" goals are contradicted by client experience. A young teenage girl's experience of social work in Alberta caused frustration and anger:

> *After they found out about the incest, after they knew what happened, the social worker came over to the house. And the social worker talked to everyone else. She talked to my father, she talked to my mother, but she never talked to me. I want to know why? – why the social worker didn't take into consideration what the victim feels like? It's like you're the one that did something wrong! You're the bad egg! And meanwhile my father gets to stay in the house and I get sent away!*

Many of the children serviced by social workers, however, are not victims of sexual or physical abuse – their main "problem" is that they happen to be poor. Most social workers would agree that welfare payments don't cover the financial costs of single parenting. But at the same time as they have this special inside knowledge, social workers are not allowed to authorize the required extra funds. This puts welfare mothers in a bind. One of them remarked:

> *Welfare comes to your home and they say "your children look undernourished" and they blame the parents. But they're the ones who don't give enough money.*

Clients and social workers know that lack of adequate income contributes to child welfare problems, and there are studies that confirm it. According to the National Council of Welfare:

> Not only are low-income children much more likely to be removed from their families, but their experience in care also tends to be more difficult. Poor kids face a greater likelihood of remaining in care for a lengthy period and ... are twice as likely as children from non-poor families to come into care more than once.[37]

Being young and Native as well as poor creates special problems.

The following observation was made by the House of Commons report on Indian Self-Government in Canada:

> Throughout the hearings, Indian witnesses condemned the policies of provincial welfare authorities for removing Indian children from reserves in cases where, in the opinion of the authorities, they were not being properly cared for by their parents. Witnesses criticized provincial authorities for judging situations by non-Indian standards, which are culturally different. The imposition of non-Indian views of child care, through the enforcement of provincial child welfare policies on reserves, has had tragic effects on Indian family life.[38]

Non-Native social workers who go to Indian reserves apply the dominant society's definition of what "child neglect" means. Consequently these social workers can end up removing an Indian child from the reserve, when according to Indian culture the child is not being neglected. Brad McKenzie, University of Manitoba, provides a case illustration of this:

> In one Indian community, a ten year old boy had been left alone for a few days, and the itinerant non-Native social worker was considering apprehension [removing the child from his home]. A community leader, concerned about the situation, asked to accompany the social worker to the home of the child. On arrival, he asked the boy to make breakfast. The boy did so, using food left for him in the refrigerator by neighbours. When asked whether he was concerned about being alone during the absence of his grandfather, the boy indicated he had easy access to neighbours, who checked up on him periodically to ensure that all was well.[39]

In this instance, the boy was not "apprehended".

But all too often a non-Native social worker will make decisions based on inadequate knowledge about Native culture. This ignorance by social workers, combined with the dominant society's racism, has left a bitter harvest:

> All of our lives we've been controlled by the larger society. Institutions, governments, organizations – they tell us how to live, how to raise our children, etc. Eventually, if someone does it for you all the time, you lose enthusiasm, motivation and individuality. For Native people, this has been termed as cultural genocide.[40]

From any child's point of view, it is a frightening and bewildering experience to be separated from parents. Social workers, emergency shelters, courts, police, foster parents, group homes, and other institutions: It becomes a maze that adds to anxiety rather than relieves it. In the case of a 12- year-old girl in Alberta who had been sexually abused by her father, both she and her younger sister were removed from their home to be placed in a foster home. A social worker took the girl and her sister to see a doctor and later a police detective. The 12-year-old recalled what happened after meeting with the police.

> *The social worker took me and my sister and we drove for a long time in the dark – I didn't know where I was going. I didn't know whether to jump out of the car and run or what. My sister didn't understand what was happening. She didn't understand what was going on or where we were going. She was getting pretty upset figuring that we were going to be taken away from home forever and everything. When we got to the foster home, the social worker told me that nobody here knows anything about what happened. She told me not to tell anybody – she said just keep everything to yourself. Nobody's supposed to know. At first I felt kind of relieved, like thinking that nobody would know. It would be a secret, but when I got there I kind of needed somebody to talk to. But there was nobody to talk to, because I was afraid if I told them I might get into trouble with the social worker.*

While the social work professional has an adult view of how it all fits together, the experience is usually one of powerlessness and confusion for the child. One child said his experience was like being a pinball-machine ball, with the buttons being pushed by the welfare system and the child bouncing from one hard place to another.

> You get all these pent-up feelings towards the system because ... you don't understand why you were taken away because then you want to see your parents but they won't let you, why are you in the place? You get all these pent-up things and you've got to take them out on someone, eh.[41]

This anger can intensify as these young girls and boys learn that the best jobs and biggest cars are reserved for other people who lead lives pointedly different than theirs. Despite a few exceptions, most of these youths won't be able to attend universities, earn high salaries, or inherit large fortunes. Yet our culture tells them "You're equal to everyone else". No wonder they become confused. Blocked by high youth unemployment, there is pressure and temptation to "turn to crime" as a way out.

Not that all such youth end up violating the law. But many do, which can result in police arrests and imprisonment in youth detention centres. Though often hired by these institutions, social workers find the agencies are often modelled upon adult prisons. From a youth in Alberta:

> This one guy said to me, "If I had my way, I'd lock up every single juvenile delinquent and throw away the key". So I don't think it's a question of helping us. I don't think they give a shit.[42]

Some of these youths will rebel against being slotted into an inferior social class. They'll rebel against a system where they see the best things reserved for others. Yet bit by bit their spirits are broken by institutions of which social workers are a part.

Similarly, institutions for the elderly provide a shock for people who have believed in the myth that our society and its institutions take care to provide for our essential well-being. For instance, an 80-year-old man who began shopping around for social and medical services to help his ailing wife visited several nursing homes:

> I found nursing homes are like institutions for people who have committed some crime. A few seemed good but in others staff were inadequate or indifferent and I felt they didn't know how to look after old people. Those places I saw had very few nurses, though they're calling them "nursing" homes. One place I went to – it was a three-storey house and I walked all over the place before I could find a staff person and she had come up from the basement. The whole place was very shabby, wallpaper peeling off the walls; people who were residents, none of them were talking, they just looked at you in a dumb sort of way.

Imagine, as well, the shock his wife was in for, as patient. This example shows, once again, the sexual dichotomy prevailing in social services. There is *his* old age and then there is *hers*. The huge majority of inmates in such nursing homes are women.

Native People: No Use for Welfare Workers?

In Saskatchewan, one study shows that over 63 per cent of male prisoners are of Indian ancestry and 85 per cent of female prisoners are of Indian ancestry. Yet the Native population of that province makes up only 10 per cent of the total population. Furthermore, a male Treaty Indian in Saskatchewan has a 70 per cent chance of being sentenced to prison at least once before reaching the age of twenty-five.[43]

Although the provinces employ many social workers who work with Native communities, the federal government has also hired professionals through its Department of Indian and Northern Affairs. That, however, is not necessarily an improvement, as the Chief and Council of the Edmonton-Hobbema District indicate: "There is no two-way communication with the Department. They come here with their programs and expect us to take them."[44]

In my experience there are a few white social workers who are the exceptions, who have developed a sensitivity to inter-cultural communication and acquired extensive knowledge and appreciation for Native culture. But more typical are these examples from Edmonton-Hobbema:

"I don't know anything about Indian people but I volunteered to work on the reserve when no other staff member would."

And: "My skin colour is different. I don't feel I should be working on the reserve and I'm so consciously aware that I'm different."

Not surprisingly, this leads to the following reaction by an Indian client: "I have no use for welfare workers because I never see them."[45]

Non-clients are also affected by the social relations shaped by the dominant society. This pits one group of Indians against another. From an Indian living on a reserve: "Welfare stinks – people should get off their asses and work."[46] Also divisive are the attitudes taught to Native students as part of their professional training. Yvonne House, a Cree educator in Saskatchewan, states:

> Schools of social work, for example, present a one-sided view based on western philosophy. It is not based on the philosophy of any number of [Indian] nations. There's limited information regarding the perspective of a tribal person. The other hindrance I see is tribal

people themselves because of the indoctrinations, brainwashing of our own classes, and racist attitudes we have ourselves.[47]

More specifically, some Indian leaders worry about what graduates from university bring back with them when they return to work on Indian reserves as employees of band councils:

> [They] come back believing that because they have a degree they have a title now. They must be treated like an elite and behave like an elite.... Now the privileged class are the fulltime employees of the band.... They are the ones who decide which changes have to take place. I really get concerned about that. They don't consult with their own members. They've decided that because they're there and they have the position and they have the training they know what the answer is. We no longer need government agents to perpetuate the colonial system. We have it within many of our own communities.[48]

Part of that colonial relationship is what happens to Indians who are clients of the welfare state. In Saskatchewan, where 64 per cent of the children in care are tribal children, Yvonne House considers that Native children have "become an industry".

> You can go to the penitentiary and find out why our men and our women have ended up in those penitentiaries. They have come from that child welfare system. Obviously that system hasn't worked. Now we have to rethink and have enough belief in who we are as [Indian] nations to try and undo over a hundred years of cultural genocide.[49]

Meanwhile the dehumanization of Native people worsens, leading to despair, alcoholism, violence, and a suicide rate much higher than the national average. Indians in larger numbers are moving to urban centres where, for many, life consists of unemployment, alcoholism, skid row, and welfare. In ways similar to gender and class, the subordination of Native people gives them a message: You are inferior. When social workers give the message: You don't deserve to be helped", they become compliant agents of the welfare state. To the client the message is: I am your jailer and you are not getting out....

Sometimes these victims turn their frustrations, anger, and rage inward, with tragic results. This happened when Nelson Small Legs Jr., an Indian leader, killed himself in May 1976. He left behind a note:

> I give up my life in protest to the present conditions concerning Indian people of southern Alberta. I also give my life in the hopes of a full-scale investigation into the dept. of Indian Affairs corruption ... and the divide and conquer tactics present on each reservation. For 100 years Indians have suffered. Must they suffer another 100 years. My suicide should open the eyes of non-Indians into how much we've suffered.[50]

This message is not reserved to Native people, or to non-whites. The overlapping characteristics of class and gender frequently interlock to intensify the subordinate and humiliating status of social work clients. When these incidents are combined with other putdowns originating from other institutions, some clients explode into violence, others sink into self-despair, others self-destruct. We then respond with alarm and call in the police – or in the case of women, more likely the psychiatrist – to deal with these "impulsive, pathological characters".

We thereby conveniently escape our own role in perpetuating the system. While that system is allowed to evade its responsibility, we make sure that the blame remains fixed upon the victim to the point where all hope seems lost.

It is at this point, then, that as social workers we must begin to reassess our own roles and the role of our profession, that we must begin to consider the relationship of social work to social change.

7

Social Work and Social Change: Fighting Back

While it is important to demand *resources,* one thing we can-
not *ask* for is new social relations: we have to make them.
London Edinburgh Weekend Return Group
In and Against the State

THE EMPHASIS OF traditional social work on the individual – both
worker and client – has made it easy for workers to ignore questions
of overall social change and difficult for them to step outside their
normal "professional" role. The practice of social work today,
based as it is on workers carrying certain caseloads of individuals
and families, means that the profession's role seems inevitably
confined to adjusting clients to prevailing social conditions – mini-
mally improving their lot perhaps, but seldom changing it. If workers push for a different way of thinking and acting in relation to clients, they are classified as "radical" and set apart from the norm.

Being confined to working through an agency with individual clients, even at out-and-out advocacy work, has its limitations. If you
get a child returned to her parents, find subsidized housing for a client, ignore superiors and cut through red tape on behalf of a person
in need of a better income, the results in the long run are often still

unsatisfactory. If you help a client receive the full amount of a welfare entitlement, that amount will still not be enough to meet the minimum standard necessary for food and housing.

Indeed, advocacy would not be needed in the first place if there were adequate provisions for aid. This is why proposals are made from time to time for a guaranteed annual income, which would create a comprehensive income floor below which no one would fall. It is unlikely, however, that such a plan could be effectively implemented unless there was also a ceiling placed on the wealth held by individuals and corporations. The real political battles will be to establish limitations on such wealth (and therefore power). We have put speed limits on our highways, but we are unwilling, so far, to see that the longer we allow the "haves" to speed up their appropriation of wealth the less there will be left over for the "have-nots".[1]

Such issues do not get addressed by social workers doing advocacy on a case-by-case basis. Jeffry Galper, author of *Social Work Practice: A Radical Perspective,* argues that making links from individual actions to the larger problems is the key to moving social work into a more effective sphere of operation, into making a contribution to movement building and structural changes. Galper emphasizes the importance of linking individual clients with other people who have similar problems, and asks social workers to consider the question: "To what extent do we encourage people to examine the more fundamental roots of the problem?"[2]

In posing this kind of question, social work moves away from its central position of implicit power over clients towards encouraging clients to take matters into their own hands by forming personal and political support groups. Through these support groups individual clients learn they are not alone in their struggles and not to blame for structural problems. The groups reduce personal isolation and make possible a degree of mutual support.

In contrast to conventional social work with groups, these support groups focus on the members' personal responses to life circumstances, as well as on the social and political roots of these circumstances. At the same time the social worker and members together can ask: How are the clients' experiences, including the social worker-client relationship, affected by the wider structures – social, political, economic, cultural – of our society? Does the very word "client" imply dependency on or subordination to the worker? Does it serve to further divide "us" from "them"? /

Ironically, the welfare state has encouraged the formation of self-help groups. This has been partly in order to save money, because agencies could get away with not hiring professionals to staff these groups. It was understood that while being autonomous, such self-help groups would essentially focus on the "self" and be limited mainly to providing emotional support to their members. Yet at times the members of these groups slipped over into political questions about the causes of their hardships. At times social workers encouraged these political questions, even at the risk of losing the limited funds provided by the state and of alienating their supervisors.

When social workers reject the strong push towards a conventional version of casework, and act forcefully in favour of clients, they are at least temporarily able to interrupt the top-down flow of power and the associated social relations imposed by the welfare state. Granted that such interruptions are by themselves insufficient to change the prevailing structures of society; they nevertheless constitute essential building blocks for basic change.

Some social workers have gone further. Pushing in new directions, they commit their particular brand of social work to the development of completely different "structures". They have done this in a number of ways, from creating new ways of working with individuals, through working with self-help groups, alternative services, and unions, to joining coalitions that include a range of social movements. Some workers, it seems, want not only to win improved services for clients but also to help build movements that will push the larger society towards fundamental change.

The Formation of Social Action Groups: A Montreal Experience

Most client groups accept the prevailing institutional arrangements as "given" and limit their function to helping members cope better within these arrangements. Examples include Alcoholics Anonymous, Parents Without Partners, or "golden age" clubs. By contrast, there are also groups of service users geared to both personal and social change. These groups range from disabled people to Native women to welfare rights advocates.

In Montreal some welfare clients developed a number of such

groups, encouraged by social workers employed mainly by community centres and settlement houses in low-income areas of the city. The social workers, including myself, were active members of these groups, but it was understood that our role would be limited to acting as advisors or resource people – an arrangement promoted by both clients and social workers.

We held informal meetings with an agenda decided by the clients, and their appraisals of their various hardships turned out to be quite different than the usual professional assessments. They told about how teachers showed obvious discrimination against their children, how landlords refused to repair broken heaters, and how in all cases there didn't seem to be anything they could do about it. The clients saw these kinds of relationships as "the problem" – as opposed to feeling that there was something inherently wrong with themselves.

As the meetings went on, our relations with clients became more personal, mutual, and voluntary than the usual worker-client relationship. We were not especially seen as "social workers" and did not advertise the fact that we were. I soon learned that clients despised social workers. They saw our profession as going about its work strictly by the book, as an institution that took children away from their homes and failed to understand what clients experience in their everyday lives. They felt that their day-by-day problems – such a big and perplexing part of their lives – were not taken seriously. It seemed to them that social workers saw those problems as trivial or as signs that the clients could not or would not look after themselves. The workers did not – or perhaps could not because of job pressures – stop to add those problems up.

By the time new clients found out that some people in the group were social workers, they had also witnessed our willingness to listen, to learn, and to be critical of social agencies. Typically, they were surprised, and more than one of them told us, "You're not like the others." In fact, we were acting in ways that were different from most social workers. Yes, we were indeed professionally on the job and we cared about the people we worked with. But we were interested, they could see, in doing more than nod our heads at their stories and make notes on bureaucratic forms.

For a short period of time a number of these groups developed, drawing in clients from different neighbourhoods. Group members began to advocate for each other at welfare offices and in the process we discovered our collective strength, which was in opposition to the individual stigma experienced by welfare recipients. One very practical result was that clients found they could increase their welfare cheques by arguing for their legal entitlements.

These client groups formed a federation, held meetings, and kept records of their decisions. One welfare recipient, Helen Bastien, volunteered to be secretary and asked me also to take minutes of a meeting so that we could compare versions afterward. Hers turned out to be more precise than mine, and I found out she had once been a bookkeeper, was now separated from her husband, and was working at home looking after her young children. The only pay available for this undervalued work was welfare.

As with welfare groups in other cities, the Montreal welfare rights group carried out a number of sit-ins and occupations of welfare offices, aimed at drawing public attention to the questionable practices of these social agencies. Some social workers joined and supported the demonstrations and some of us helped to plan them. When it came to talking with the media, the workers took care to respect the emerging leadership of welfare recipients, who acted as spokespersons for the groups.

We carried out one action that was both serious and fun. It came about after the groups had requested permission to set up information booths in the waiting rooms of the welfare offices. The welfare department said no. So one bright morning, three welfare activists walked up one flight of stairs into a welfare office, carrying a portable cardtable, a pitcher of hot coffee, paper cups, and a stack of information booklets. They set up the table in the waiting area and proceeded to offer coffee and information to other clients waiting for appointments.

A well-dressed administrator soon popped out of an office cubicle and asked the three "outsiders" to leave and take their things with them. They said they'd rather stay, and continued to offer coffee and information. In a huff the administrator retreated into his cubicle and presumably phoned the welfare director, who presumably called the police.

I was with a second group of people waiting in a parked car, motor running, across the street from the welfare office. In the car we had a walkie-talkie that kept us in continuous contact with our three people inside. Those of us in the car were to serve as lookouts for the police. Sure enough, half an hour after our people had first gone into the welfare office, we heard sirens and saw a number of rather large, white-helmeted policemen riding majestically into view on their motorcycles. We felt like comedians in a movie, waiting to tip off a casino about an imminent raid.

We radioed to our friends inside and told them the police were on their way. Our inside people thereupon closed up their portable table, took their coffee pitcher, said goodbye to the other clients, and started down the stairs towards the street. The police were by that time making their way up the stairs, where they met three courteous, neatly-dressed, harmless-looking people coming down. The three gave greetings to the police, who smiled back and kept climbing the stairs. The last officer patiently held the door open to help our friends exit onto the street. Now all the police were inside and our friends came across the street, hopped into our car, and off we went to another welfare office for a repeat performance.

Social Action Groups as Building Blocks

Although client groups have rocked the boat, does this approach offer promise for social change? Gary Cameron, a social worker active with these groups in Montreal, offers a sobering observation:

> Most social action organizations do not survive. Their average lifespan is probably about five years. Those that do survive are barely recognizable as social action organizations. A multi-issue, mass-based organization has proved to be exceedingly difficult to maintain.[3]

In addition to a possibly limited life-span, social action groups face a new dilemma when they do succeed in producing reforms. Feminist writer and activist Charlotte Bunch refers to this problem in the context of the women's liberation movement:

> Unless we are determined to prevent it, reforms most often enhance the privilege of a few at the expense of the many. Unless good political education accompanies work on a reform, success can lead to the conclusion that the system works or failure can lead to cynicism about women's ability to bring about change.[4]

Equally disturbing is a critique by York University professor Howard Buchbinder, who points out that even when social workers become militant and their demands seem harsh, their practice is still biased towards modifications that are within the range of the present political or social system. The implication, according to Buchbinder, is that given "enough momentum" based on community pressures, "all problems are resolvable within the system".[5]

It is true that once client groups are organized, many of their demands – for example, more government funding for a community centre, or changes to specific social legislation – can be accommodated by the state and social agencies, usually after considerable resistance. Such accommodation does not alter the basic relations of power, a fact frequently obscured by the minor concessions that are granted. Where does that leave client groups that opt for social action? Are social workers who support such groups inevitably limited to working for superficial changes?

When client groups develop their personal and political interests in a direction that leads to social action, many clients and professionals stumble onto a discovery. We realize, perhaps for the first time, that there are many others in similar positions who are also angry with receiving the short end of the stick. We discover that as a group we can break the silence, name our experiences, and explore group action. During the Montreal experience I felt personally empowered because I too could begin naming and talking about the forces trying to censor my actions: for example, the social agency's board members, who wanted to eliminate the social action efforts by the agency in order to concentrate solely on more research of social problems.

Very frequently such group actions are diametrically opposed to the "normal" flow of power within the welfare state. When social workers join client groups involved in social action there are implications for their practice. As Gary Cameron puts it, "The social action perspective insists that as social workers confront the inevitable shortages of resources, they put pressure upwards in the system rather than downwards on clients to accept their fate."[6] Of course such power reversals in isolated instances won't by themselves produce social transformation, just as case advocacy within social agencies won't by itself transform these agencies. Yet just as in case advocacy, social action groups form essential building blocks to basic change.

For one thing, the key ingredient of this type of social work, opposition to the existing flow of top-down power, creates the potential for change in the personal consciousness of the individuals involved. It is no accident that when social workers and service recipients carry out oppositional work there are ample opportunities for an expansion of critical consciousness about what makes society unjust, and certainly many more opportunities than conventional social work practice provides.

Much also depends on the accessibility of a critical analysis that better explains why things happen the way they do. Such alternative analysis can then be tested in the crucible of group actions. The testing process is itself a personal and political struggle because most of us have been indoctrinated into a series of myths that help to uphold, rather than challenge, the present social system. Nevertheless, through such a process groups have transformed themselves from being a conventional pressure group to an organization committed to the radical restructuring of society.[7]

The Role of Alternative Services

While social action groups make forceful demands on the political and bureaucratic systems for delivery of new and more effective resources – often hoping that this action will lead to more fundamental change – alternative services attempt to institutionalize new forms of social relations: establishing a shelter for battered women, a crisis phone line, a drop-in and information centre, or a Native-controlled community centre. This is what the authors of *In and Against the State* refer to as *making* new social relations.[8]

Alternative services usually spring from the work of a specific oppressed community or movement: women, Native people, ethnic and visible minorities, gays and lesbians, local tenants' groups, the disabled, or ex-psychiatric patients. They emphasize the principle of community control over professional services. Tenants, for example, have at times formed organizations to counter the power of landlords; these tenant organizations focus on solving problems in specific buildings, perhaps, or on working for new legislation and policies. As an alternative, potential tenants have formed or joined housing co-operatives where governing bodies are elected from project residents who thereby obtain a strong voice in decisions about their housing.

Alternative services in other areas may emphasize the importance of acknowledging and dealing with the immense prejudice against their constituencies. Services to gays and lesbians, for example, include public education about the extensive discrimination faced by people who are continuously subjected to models of "normalcy" that deny and reject sexual diversity.[9] So too the prejudice against visible minorities has prompted the emergence of services and networks that provide alternatives to bureaucratic institutions.

The services of the various movements or communities strive to develop relationships based on equality – whether between the providers and receivers of service, or among co-ordinators and staff. The women's movement has been especially influential in developing non-hierarchical approaches to organizing and delivering feminist services. Many of the newer services are organized as co-ops or collectives so that staff co-operatively make major decisions, often with essential input from the users of the service. Staff and sometimes users – not management – have a major say in hiring. The services are often staffed and co-ordinated by people rooted in the particular community being served, people who are personally committed to the reduction or elimination of structural inequalities. They tend to have a shared analysis of what causes the problems and what creates the need for their services.

The women's movement has also contributed basic principles of counselling that counteract the traditional approaches to providing service. Helen Levine summarizes the role of feminist counselling:

> It has to do with an approach, a feminist way of defining women's struggles and facilitating change. It is no mysterious, professional technique. The focus is on women helping women in a non-hierarchical, reciprocal and supportive way.... It rests on a critical analysis of the sexism embedded in the theory and practice of the helping professions.[10]

Feminist analysis also emphasizes the centrality of joining the personal and political dimensions of sexism. It connects, for instance, the sexual division of paid and unpaid labour in and beyond the home with its impact on self-esteem and interpersonal relationships. Feminists see an understanding and a linking of both dimensions – the personal and the political – as crucial in bringing about significant change.

Similarly, social workers who are involved with efforts of indigenous people to protect their culture and restore their autonomy find that they too are connecting the personal with the political. In his study of social work and Native people, Brad McKenzie cites an example in Manitoba, where steps are being taken to increase Native control over social services and social work:

> There are resident Native workers on each reserve, and every community has a Child and Family Service Committee composed of selected community service providers, elders and other respected community members. Committees have a mandate which includes the provision of advice and direction to child welfare workers.... It is not uncommon for committee members to participate in developing specific plans for dealing with a family concern, then sharing responsibility with the local worker for carrying out aspects of the intervention plan.... Extended family members are used as the first alternative resource if substitute care is required. Community foster homes have been developed according to community standards; in one tribal council composed of eight reserves, approximately one hundred new foster homes were approved during the first two years of the Native-controlled system.[11]

In this way the traditional walls between the providers and the receivers are considerably reduced, if not eliminated altogether.

The process of moving towards structures of equality and shared power has special relevance to social work, traditionally viewed as a woman's profession with mostly women practitioners and clients. "Women have always served others and have been told that their glory and fulfillment is to be found in the denial of themselves," Angela Miles writes. Caring has been used against women to keep them trapped and silenced. But caring can have a liberating potential. According to Angela Miles:

> Women's service has not been only forced service to their masters, it has been also the caring and nurturing of each other and our children. It has been the building and maintenance of the social connections and commitment that embody what is human in our society. It extends far beyond what is forced from women as subordinates to become in many cases freely chosen expressions of love and support which are not the self-denial but the expression of women's selves in the world. At the same time as it has oiled the wheels of an oppressive system and eased the lot of our rulers, women's service has kept alive an alternative, and in part subversive, set of values and ways of life.[12]

It is this form of service, not based on self-denial but rather on feminism's alternative vision, that inspires alternative services. There is a rejection of the dominant ideology, reinforced by conventional social agencies, which first defines clients as inadequate and / or pathological "cases", and then puts forth professional "expertise" to rehabilitate, to "normalize" individuals and families into conformity with prevailing patterns.

By contrast, social movements offer a different view of personal problems, seeing unequal power relations and unequal material resources as the source of the problem. Social movements and their alternative services are indeed subversive. They are in conflict with the services and objectives of conventional social agencies. But most important, instead of helping to legitimate society's undemocratic structures and institutions they are committed to exposing and fundamentally changing them.

Alternative Services: Issues and Pitfalls

Just as the dominant society's version of conventional social services has become an instrument for the perpetuation of inequality, when social services become part of potentially transformative communities, these services become oppositional and their staff become part of the struggle for basic change. Part of that struggle occurs through outreach and consciousness-raising activities.

Jillian Ridlington notes the changed political climate and the more sophisticated analysis used by feminists, based on a decade of trying to change things on shoestring budgets and realizing the changes were only bandaids. She writes:

> There is a chasm now between the women we have become and the women who need feminist services. They come from a perspective that was once our own, but which our vision now tells us is obscured – we can no longer see the world as non-feminists still see it. Their needs are those of our more innocent selves: support, a chance to exchange experiences with other women; information, which may lead to insights and autonomy.[13]

This can serve as a caution against the trap of arrogance. Having developed a critical awareness, we can become self-righteous and forget the importance of listening to, learning from, and sharing with the very groups we see as most oppressed.

When some alternative services become viable, grow, and gain credibility, they face a new challenge. They want to hire more staff, possibly including social workers, but that requires money. So they draw up proposals and submit them to various branches of government or to an agency such as the United Way, asking for funding and realizing the risk of co-optation. Cindy Player describes the dilemma with reference to abused women and their children: "We desperately need funding in order to provide necessary support and shelter for women and children. But far too often, the strings attached to that funding run counter to our feminist philosophy."[14]

When governments find they can't control the alternative services, funds are eventually cut or eliminated. Vancouver's Transition House, which had offered refuge and support for hundreds of battered women, was forced to close when the provincial government moved to the political right and withdrew funding. For its users, this meant reverting to the traditional services such as the Salvation Army and the welfare department.

Given the enormous difficulties in working either within traditional agencies or within alternative services, some social workers have opted for a form of private practice that rejects the corporate and hierarchical models. These social workers sell their services on the assumption that the selling of a service is not in and of itself exploitative, just as food co-ops sell food and publishing collectives sell books without necessarily becoming capitalist or sexist. It depends on the kinds of social relations generated by the effort. Progressive social workers in private practice ideally commit themselves to an egalitarian and democratic approach, which they apply to their own organizational structures as well as to their interactions with clients. In addition they get essential social nourishment and new ideas from their personal and political roots in one or more of the grassroots movements.

Such practitioners, however, don't have it easy because of the inevitable shortages of funds. Furthermore, the area is full of contradictions, as reflected in efforts to develop egalitarian and non-oppressive relations with service users, while working as a professional entrepreneur. It becomes easy either to slip back into the traditional medical model that divides the user from the service provider, or to become more interested in business profitability than user well-being.

Alternative services, then, clearly have their limitations. In the end the services they provide will not alone promote the goal of basic change. Yet these services do make an essential contribution. They illustrate through direct, everyday experience that radically different kinds of services are feasible, practical, and more personally satisfying than practice within conventional institutions. They become prototypes for the alternative institutions of the future, providing us with positive, hopeful glimpses of what might be and practical lessons on how to get there.

Unions and Social Work

It is well known that, historically, labour unions have struggled for better working conditions and pay. Perhaps less well known are the efforts by the labour movement to urge governments to develop social programs such as old age pensions, unemployment insurance, and medicare. These social programs would not have been established if labour had not pressed for them through the political arena. During periods when these programs come under attack it is, again, the labour movement, along with others, that organizes opposition to the cutbacks.

Most social workers belong to unions, because most of us are employed at workplaces that have been unionized. Within provincial governments, one union covers all or a large part of the public service. In Newfoundland, social workers employed by the province belong to the Newfoundland Association of Public Employees (NAPE); in Quebec, they belong to La Confédération des Syndicats Nationaux; in Ontario it is the Ontario Public Service Employees' Union (OPSEU); and in Alberta it is the Alberta Union of Public Employees (AUPE).

The advantage of being part of a larger union is that member social workers benefit from the strength of the larger group and the collective agreements it achieves. Unionization, especially in the public sector, has raised salaries for social workers, although the government sometimes rolls back these gains through contracting-out. For example, the federal government offered to pay the John Howard Society (a non-profit, voluntary agency) to carry out parole work that would otherwise be done by the federal parole service.

While such moves are ostensibly to save money, they effectively undermine the job security and improved working conditions that federal parole officers have won through collective agreements.

Unions have not, however, always delivered what social workers hoped for, even where social workers formed their own social work union. John Melichercik, who examined the collective agreements between social workers and the Children's Aid societies throughout Ontario, concludes:

> It is not infrequent for individual social workers in unionized agencies to say that what they were really hoping to achieve was, not higher salaries or longer vacations, but a greater or more meaningful role in the development and implementation of service programs, and generally in increasing their participation in the administration of the agencies.[15]

Melichercik found that the collective agreements covered the usual bread and butter issues, that is, salaries, grievance procedures, and other conditions of work, and that unionization did not lead to a greater participation by social workers in the decision-making processes of these agencies.

The difficulty of achieving greater democracy in the workplace is consistent with the standard power relations nourished by the welfare state. Unions, as Jeffry Galper points out, are not necessarily socialist organizations aiming at radical changes in political structures.[16] Often unions have organized themselves like business enterprises, with power concentrated at the top of male-dominated hierarchies. Galper states:

> They do not raise the question of private ownership of the means of production by their very existence. In this sense they accept capitalism and even facilitate its smooth functioning. At the same time, they represent workers organizing as workers to challenge the power and ability of capitalists, or in the case of social service workers to challenge the power and the ability of the state to control wages and conditions of work.[17]

Although unions are recognized as being among the most democratic of our institutions – with rank and file participation a visible priority on convention floors or in meeting halls – feminists have criticized them not only as male-dominated organizations, but also for being preoccupied with product rather than process, and for avoiding women's needs and issues. As Denise Kouri states, "Fighting for women's issues inevitably means fighting for rank and file control of unions, because that is where women are, and rank and file control is what is needed to change trade union policies."[18]

Confronted – directly and indirectly – by the women's movement, the union movement has become much more involved in the struggle for equal pay for work of equal value, day care, maternity leave, pensions for older women, paid child care leave, sexual harassment, and other issues initiated by women. Sandy Fox argues, "That linking of broader issues to the more traditional economic concerns of union conventions was the result of a lot of hard work by union activists with the help and support of feminists outside the union movement."[19]

For social workers, women as well as men, unions can become forums for challenging the inadequacies of social programs. Unions have, for example, attacked the abysmally low levels of "income maintenance" provided by provincial governments. They have criticized the role of businesses working for profit in the delivery of social services (in the running of nursing homes, or private boarding houses for former mental patients, for instance).[20] OPSEU has critiqued the Ontario Ministry of Community and Social Services for restructuring its social programs and moving towards a "complete automated social service model". Its pamphlet *Insider Report* argues that while the Ministry contends that this new direction is for "greater efficiency", the trend is clearly towards less service.[21] The report documents how social work clients receive short shrift from provincial social agencies, and concludes that there is a "fundamental contradiction between the Ministry's stated policy objectives and the programs designed to implement these policies".[22] When social workers support such critiques, they realize that the criticism is being levelled at the system and its decision-makers rather than at those workers who are expected to implement such decisions.

Unions are more recent arrivals in the voluntary sector. Although in most cases they have learned to live with unions, many agency directors prefer what they remember as the collegial patterns of communication, prior to unionization. Such perceptions are often reinforced by the business people who sit on the agency's voluntary board and who develop alliances with the agency management. Having recognized such dynamics, some labour organizations are beginning to press for labour representation on the boards of these voluntary agencies.

In one survey of child welfare agencies, directors were asked whether there had been improvements in organizational functioning since unionization.[23] In most areas the answer was "no change" or "deterioration". A minority of directors, the survey found, had positive attitudes to unions. By contrast, a significant majority of front-line workers were in favour of unions after several years of working in a unionized agency; even though before unionization these workers had been evenly divided positive and neutral in their attitudes to unions.[24]

This worker support is not surprising. Although collective agreements have not addressed the issue of worker participation in decision-making on agency policy, they do bring increased job security, aided partly by the establishment of grievance procedures. This creates in turn increased power or control for the worker: a small but important achievement. Job security becomes a critical advantage when social workers decide to support alternative services through their own jobs, or when they begin to engage in social action with client groups. And the labour movement's emphasis on solidarity and collective engagement with other workers in general casts the role of social workers into a broader context. It encourages both reflection and analysis of wider issues and the formation of important links with other movements and other workers.

Coalitions

It is still not enough for social work to do advocacy for and with individuals, to form social action groups, establish alternative services, or join unions. If social work is to make a contribution to progressive social change, a key step is for social workers to make connections with social movements that have similar concerns and goals.

Even with those movements that appear to be distant from the concerns of social work – such as those focusing on environmental or Third World issues, or nuclear disarmament – it is possible to identify common interests. These interests include everything from working to optimize human dignity and to reconstruct society on a basis of mutual respect; to making sure a country's natural resources are safeguarded for the good of all; or to seeing that militarism and military spending do not determine the direction of public spending.

In fact, social workers and social movements have a reciprocal need for each other. It is ineffective – and damaging – for social workers to work in isolation. At the same time social workers, through their jobs, have daily contact with people who constitute a specific or potential subgroup of larger social movements. Through a variety of such contacts, social workers can provide movements with concrete opportunities to expand *within* their own constituencies and also to form coalitions *across* constituencies based on common interests.

The subgroups, as Mariana Valverde points out, form a necessary beginning in the process of organizing:

> Immigrant women ... have to be organized as immigrant women, and *then* plug into the women's movement. It would be very alienating for individual immigrant women to join a group that was primarily anglo. They need their own groups, which fight for specifically immigrant women's issues and identify their own concerns, so that when they come into the general women's movement they can set their own demands. Similarly lesbians or native women, or any woman who faces a separate oppression, needs her own organizations and her own groups.[25]

With these specific concerns as a starting point, common actions will emerge. The Mulroney Conservative government offered a good example of this. When Brian Mulroney ran for prime minister he clearly promised no cutbacks in social programs at the federal level – talking about a "sacred trust" between the government and the people. Yet shortly after he assumed office in 1984 his government's first budget contradicted his campaign message: Pensions of older people would be cut. In response, groups of older people pulled together via their grassroots organizations and spearheaded a coalition that included labour, feminist, and religious organizations. Numerous social workers became involved, helping to organize public education campaigns and mobilize public protests. As a result of this powerful coalition, the Conservatives retreated.

Similarly, coalitions have emerged around demonstrations by welfare recipients, indigenous peoples, tenants' groups, and the unemployed. These groups have received moral and material support from unions, women's organizations, church groups, and progressive people within other institutions and professions.

Unfortunately, very frequently social action by one constituency fails to attract much material support from others – partly because each movement is primarily struggling with its own specific agenda and partly because these struggles lead to differing goals for mass organizing.

When social workers do participate in social movements and their coalitions, their role provides a sharp contrast to the perspectives and actions encouraged by the managers of the welfare state. This in turn provides other social workers with alternative models of practice. Eric Shragge, who teaches social work at McGill University, writes:

> Posters, newspapers, announcements of meetings, and worker initiated speakers from outside groups can help build solidarity between workers, clients, and social movements. Although not overcoming the problem of technocratic control, this approach does bring the broader social struggles closer to clients and social workers, with the effect of breaking down a false consensus between social workers and management.[26]

Such a climate of opposition within social agencies also serves to clarify the congruence of interests between unions, front-line workers, and users of social services. A further step is for social workers to highlight the question of client well-being on the agendas of their unions and agencies.

This is a far cry from social workers being engaged in pressure group politics or polite lobbying pursued on the basis that the state is neutral and that existing social structures are legitimate. Our participation in small or large demonstrations of opposition has an impact on our personal lives that underlines the need for mass action. As Sandy Fox illustrates, feminists have been in the forefront of linking consciousness-raising to mass action:

> Mass action can mean anything from ten women or people on a picket line to thousands of people on a street; it means people who

are putting their foot on the sidewalk or on the road to protest something – not begging or saying please give us something, but demanding their rights. A demonstration is inspiring because it means that
lots of other people share our concerns; it means that we're not
speaking alone, that there are other people who feel the same things
we do. And that's why the state's so afraid of demonstrations –
because it gives people a sense of their collective strength.[27]

The challenge is for social workers (and others) to participate in
mass actions that combine the strength of several social movements.
Such coalition-building across movements does not mean homogen-
izing all specific grievances, injustices, and oppressions into one
uniform blob. On the contrary, the strength and vitality of such
coalitions depend on the capacity of each social movement to retain
its autonomy, analysis, and goals. To the extent that different movements learn from each other, enrich their own analysis, and gain
from the insights and experiences of others struggling in different
ways against oppressive structures, such a process strengthens
rather than weakens the forces of progressive change.

Understandably, feminists are suspicious of calls for coalitions
with, for example, the peace movement: Will the coalition result in
feminist issues being shelved until after the world is safe from a
nuclear holocaust? Will women be used once more to serve the
needs of others while their own oppression is ignored? So, too, the
labour movement has its own fears: How many jobs will be lost if
war-related industries are forced to go out of business? Native
people's organizations are suspicious about joining larger coalitions
with whites: Will Native claims and concerns again be swept under
the rug?

These fears are grounded in the history and experience of the
particular constituencies. To be effective, coalitions have to respond
to them. Potential members have to be reassured that their vital
interests and autonomy will be respected, and that joining a coalition does not mean assimilation and absorption into someone else's
cause. The coalition has to be flexible enough, democratic enough,
to adapt to the specific requirements and needs of each of the
member-movements or groups. In turn each movement has to take
responsibility for clarifying its own ground rules for participation
and for building a non-oppressive relationship within the coalition.
Each constituency has to make sure that its own agenda is out in the

open and that any possible conflicts with the coalition agenda are discussed.

These new social relations prefigure the alternative future we wish to build. To the extent that social work actions support and strengthen this process, such actions would be motivated by altruism of a different stripe than that which pervades the profession today. A genuine caring for others necessarily includes action based on a personal and political awareness of the root causes of social inequalities. This action works to reclaim the meaning of human dignity and human equality by refusing the conformity prescribed by managers of the welfare state.

In this process, our activism within the women's liberation movement, the labour movement, Native people's organizations, the peace movement, and other social networks becomes crucial. Each of these movements contributes to coalitions in solidarity with other segments of the population – people blocked from power and decision-making regarding the direction of our society. When all of these blocked segments are added together, the sum becomes an overwhelming majority of the public. In joining this movement of solidarity, we will be confronting the walls that prevent both personal and political transformation. Such transformation necessarily demands a basic redistribution of power – so that the practice of democracy comes within the reach of everyone, rather than being manipulated by those who now dominate the heights of our political and social structures.

Notes

Chapter 1: Social Work and Public Conscience

1 For recent reports based on Statistics Canada figures, see *The Toronto Star,* July 10, 1986, p. 1; and *The Globe and Mail,* July 10, 1986, p. 1; where official figures put the "poor" at one in five Canadian households and indicate that the average Canadian income was in decline from 1982 to 1984; meanwhile "The top 1 per cent of families – earning an average $212,000 a year – are getting richer and will likely continue to do so" *(Toronto Star).*

2 Jennifer Dale and Peggy Foster, *Feminists and State Welfare* (London: Routledge & Kegan Paul, 1986), p. 96.

3 See, for example, *The Canadian Encyclopedia* (Edmonton: Hurtig, 1985), "The Welfare State," p. 1930.

4 Ian Gough, *The Political Economy of the Welfare State* (London: Macmillan, 1979), p. 12.

5 James B. Davies, "The 1970 Survey of Consumer Finance Non-Sampling Error and the Personal Distribution of Wealth in Canada," in Economic Council of Canada, *Reflections on Canadian Incomes* (Ottawa: Ministry of Supply and Services, 1980). p. 329.

6 City of Toronto, Dept. of Public Health, *The Unequal Society: A Challenge to Public Health* (Toronto, 1985), pp. 2, 3, 5.

7 John Porter, *The Vertical Mosaic: An Analysis of Social Class and Power in Canada* (Toronto: University of Toronto Press, 1965), p. 264.

8 Jane Ursel, "The State and the Maintenance of Patriarchy: A Case Study of Family, Labour and Welfare Legislation in Canada," in James Dickinson and Bob Russell (eds.), *Family, Economy & State: The Social Reproduction Process Under Capitalism* (Toronto: Garamond Press, 1986), p. 150.

9 Dorothy E. Smith, "Women, Class and Family," in Varda Burstyn and Dorothy Smith, *Women, Class, Family and the State* (Toronto: Garamond Press, 1985), p. 2.

10 Margrit Eichler, "The Connection Between Paid and Unpaid Labour," in Paula Bourne (ed.), *Women's Paid and Unpaid Work: Historical and Contemporary Perspectives* (Toronto: New Hogtown Press, 1985), p. 63.

11 *United Nations Report,* 1980.

12 Wallace Clement, *The Canadian Corporate Elite: An Analysis of Economic Power* (Toronto: McClelland and Stewart, 1975).

13 Ibid., p. 2.

14 Mary O'Brien, "Feminist Praxis," in Angela R. Miles and Geraldine Finn (eds.), *Feminism in Canada: From Pressure to Politics* (Montreal: Black Rose, 1982), pp. 265-266.

15 Ibid., p. 254.

16 Todd Gitlin, *The Whole World is Watching: Mass Media in the Making and Unmaking of the New Left* (Berkeley: University of California Press, 1980), p. 9.

17 Ibid., p. 10.

18 Barb Thomas and Charles Novogrodsky, *Combatting Racism in the Workplace: Readings Kit* (Toronto: Cross Cultural Communications Centre, 1983), p. 17.

19 B. Singh Bolaria and Peter Li, *Racial Oppression in Canada* (Toronto: Garamond Press, 1985), p. 181.

Chapter 2: The Roots of Social Work: Early Attitudes

1 Statute cited by Karl de Schweinitz, *England's Road to Social Security* (New York: Barnes, 1943), pp. 21-22.

2 Mary Daly, *Gyn / Ecology: The Metaethics of Radical Feminism* (Boston: Beacon Press, 1978), p. 180.

3 Ibid., pp. 178-222.

4 Quoted in de Schweinitz, *England's Road,* p. 26; see also W. Friedlander and R. Apte, *Introduction to Social Welfare* (Englewood Cliffs, N.J.: Prentice-Hall, 1980), pp. 9-18.

5 Don Bellamy, "Social Welfare in Canada," in *Encyclopedia of Social Work* (New York: National Association of Social Workers, 1965), p. 37.

6 Ibid.

7 Dennis Guest, *The Emergence of Social Security in Canada* (Vancouver: University of British Columbia, 1980), p. 12.

8 Pat Thane, "Women and the Poor Law in Victorian and Edwardian England," in *History Workshop,* Issue 6, Autumn 1978, p. 31.

9 David Macarov, *The Design of Social Welfare* (New York: Holt, Rinehart & Winston, 1978), pp. 191-200; see also Ashley Montagu, *On Being Human* (New York: Hawthorn, 1966).

10 S. Marcus, "Their Brothers' Keepers," in Willard Gaylin et al., *Doing Good: The Limits of Benevolence* (New York: Pantheon, 1978), p. 51.

11 Quoted in de Schweinitz, *England's Road,* p. 123.

12 Ibid.

13 Philip Corrigan and Val Corrigan, "State Formation and Social Policy until 1871," in Noel Parry, Michael Rustin, and Carol Satyamurti, *Social Work, Welfare and the State* (Beverly Hills: Sage, 1980), p. 14.

14 Dale and Foster, *Feminists and State Welfare,* p. 34.

15 By 1882 there were 92 social agencies in the U.S. modelled after the British C.O.S. These were the forerunners of the Family Service Associations now found in many U.S. and Canadian locations. See P. Popple, "Contexts of Practice," in A. Rosenblatt and D. Waldvogel (eds.), *Handbook of Clinical Social Work* (San Francisco: Jossey-Bass, 1983), p. 75; see also Bernard Lappin, "Stages in the Development of Community Organization Work as a Social Work Method," Ph.D. diss., School of Social Work, University of Toronto, 1965, p. 64. Lappin's thesis provides an excellent overview of the C.O.S. and early Settlement House movements. Another useful source focusing on the history of social welfare is Friedlander and Apte, *Introduction to Social Welfare,* chapters 2 and 3.

16 Quoted in Roy Lubove, *Professional Altruist* (Boston: Harvard, 1965), p. 13.

17 Lappin, "Stages," p. 64.

18 Dale and Foster, *Feminists and State Welfare*, p. 38.

19 Quoted in Guest, *The Emergence of Social Security*, p. 80.

20 Terry Copp, *The Anatomy of Poverty: The Condition of the Working Class in Montreal 1907-1929* (Toronto: McClelland and Stewart, 1974), p. 106.

21 Ibid.

22 Quoted in ibid., p. 115.

23 Quoted in Guest, *The Emergence of Social Security*, p. 57. Charlotte Whitton also opposed family allowances, which were nevertheless introduced in 1944. See Brigitte Kitchen, "Wartime Social Reform: The Introduction of Family Allowances," *Canadian Journal of Social Work Education,* Vol. 7, No. 1, 1981, pp. 29-54.

24 Copp, *The Anatomy of Poverty,* p. 127. On the growth of the welfare state, see also: Allan Irving, "Canadian Fabians: The Work and Thought of Harry Cassidy and Leonard Marsh, 1930-1945," *Canadian Journal of Social Work Education,* Vol. 7, No. 1, 1981, pp. 7-28; James Struthers, *No Fault of their Own: Unemployment and the Canadian Welfare State, 1914-1941* (Toronto: University of Toronto Press, 1983); and a special issue on "Leonard Marsh, Social Welfare Pioneer," in *Journal of Canadian Studies,* Vol. 21, No. 2, Summer 1986, especially Allan Moscovitch, "The Welfare State Since 1975" for more recent developments.

25 Canada, House of Commons, *Minutes of the Proceedings of the Special Committee on Indian Self-Government,* Issue No. 40, Oct. 12, 1983, Oct. 20, 1983.

26 Quoted in Alvin Finkel, "Origins of the welfare state in Canada," in Leo Panitch (ed.), *The Canadian State: Political Economy and Political Power* (Toronto: University of Toronto Press, 1977), p. 349.

27 Quoted in Peter Findlay, "The 'Welfare State' and the State of Welfare in Canada," paper presented at Annual Conference of Canadian Association of Schools of Social Work, Ottawa, 1982, p. 9.

28 Dennis Guest, "Social Security," in *Canadian Encyclopedia,* p. 1723.

29 Glenn Drover, "Social Work," in *Canadian Encyclopedia,* p. 1724. Note that these numbers must be distinguished from the smaller number of social workers who have joined provincial social work associations (see Chapter 4).

30 Joanne C. Turner and Francis J. Turner (eds.), *Canadian Social Welfare* (Toronto: Collier Macmillan, 1981), p. 3.

31 Wanda Bernard, Lydia Lucas-White, and Dorothy Moore, "Two Hands tied behind her Back; the Dual Negative Status of 'Minority Group'

Women," paper presented to CASSW Annual Conference, Dalhousie University, June 1981, p. 17.

32 Ibid.

33 Saul D. Alinsky, *Reveille for Radicals* (Chicago: University of Chicago, 1946), p. 82; quoted in Bryan M. Knight, "Poverty in Canada," in Dimitrios L. Roussopoulos (ed.), *Canada and Social Change* (Montreal: Black Rose, 1973), p. 23.

34 Copp, *The Anatomy of Poverty*, p. 127.

Chapter 3: Schools of Altruism

1 Figures from the Secretariat of the Canadian Association of Schools of Social Work, Ottawa, 1986.

2 Joan Turner, "There Comes a Time," in Joan Turner and Lois Emery (eds.), *Perspectives on Women in the 1980s* (Winnipeg: University of Manitoba, 1983), p. 8.

3 Ibid.

4 L. Davis, "Black and White Social Work Faculty: Perceptions of Respect, Satisfaction, and Job Permanence," *Journal of Sociology and Social Welfare*, Vol. XII, No. 1, March 1985, pp. 79-94.

5 See Montagu, *On Being Human*, pp. 27-46.

6 Erich Fromm, *The Art of Loving* (New York: Bantam, 1956), pp. 50, 19.

7 Policy, Planning and Information Branch, Dept. of National Health and Welfare, *Inventory of Income Security Programs, July 1985* (Ottawa, 1986), p. 16.

8 See, for instance, John A. Crane, "Employment of Social Service Graduates in Canada," a study carried out by the Canadian Association of Schools of Social Work, Ottawa, 1974, p. 89. This study was based on a sample of 552 graduates and found that more than 91 per cent of graduates were practising in the area of casework or groupwork, whereas only 5 per cent were practising in planning, policy, or administrative roles only. This study also found that graduates were spending most of their time on problems of family relationships or emotional health, or child placement or child care.

9 Betty J. Piccard, *An Introduction to Social Work*, 3rd edition (Homewood, Illinois: Dorsey, 1983), p. 43.

10 Mary E. Richmond, *Social Diagnosis* (New York: The Free Press, 1917), p. 25.

11 See Florence Hollis, "Social Casework: The Psychosocial Approach," in *Encyclopedia of Social Work,* Vol. 2 (Washington: National Association of Social Workers, 1977), pp. 1300-1308.

12 C. Germain and A. Gitterman, *The Life Model of Social Work Practice* (New York: Columbia University, 1980), pp. 5, 6. These authors define their life model as consisting of ecological perspective, conceptual framework, practice method, and their view of social work's social purpose (p. 1).

13 Lawrence Shulman, *The Skills of Helping Individuals and Groups* (Itasca, Illinois: Peacock, 1979), p. 11.

14 Lubove, *Professional Altruist,* p. 13.

15 Martin Loney, "A political economy of citizen participation," in Panitch (ed.), *The Canadian State,* p. 447.

16 Ibid.

17 Ruby Pernell, "Social Work Values on the New Frontiers," in D.S. Sanders, O. Kurren and J. Fischer (eds.), *Fundamentals of Social Work Practice: A Book of Readings* (Belmont, Cal.: Wadsworth, 1982), p. 23.

18 Quoted in Lappin, "Stages," p. 174.

19 Quoted in Lappin, "Stages," p. 73.

20 Quoted in *Social Welfare* XIV, No. 6, March 1932, pp. 117, 119.

21 Elspeth Latimer, "An Analysis of the Social Action Behaviour of the Canadian Association of Social Workers, From Its Organizational Beginnings to the Modern Period," Ph.D. diss., Faculty of Social Work, University of Toronto, 1972, p. 315.

22 Richard Cloward and Frances Fox Piven, "Notes Toward a Radical Social Work," in R. Bailey and M. Drake (eds.), *Radical Social Work* (New York: Pantheon, 1976), p. xv. The social control inherent in systems theory is also examined by Ramesh Mishra, *Society and Social Policy: Theories and Practice of Welfare,* 2nd ed. (London: Macmillan, 1985), pp. 54-55.

23 Allen Pincus and Anne Minahan, *Social Work Practice: Model and Method* (Itasca, Illinois: Peacock, 1973), pp. 4, 5.

24 Ibid., p. 8.

25 Helen Levine, "The Personal Is Political: Feminism and the Helping Professions," in Miles and Finn, *Feminism in Canada,* p. 200.

26 Ivan Illich et al., *Disabling Professions* (London: Marion Boyars, 1977), pp. 27, 17.

Chapter 4: Social Workers: On the Front Line

1 Latimer, "An Analysis," pp. 52 and 84 for the 1966 and 1939 figures respectively. The 1986 figure was obtained from Mary Hegan, executive director, Canadian Association of Social Workers, based upon the following membership in provincial social work professional associations in 1986: Newfoundland 156; Nova Scotia 252; P.E.I. 51; New Brunswick 95; Quebec 2,145; Ontario 3,883; Manitoba 209; Saskatchewan 241; Alberta 978; British Columbia 1,314 – for a total of 9,324.

2 Canadian Association of Social Workers, *Code of Ethics* (1983), p. 1.

3 John McKnight, "Professionalized Service and Disabling Help," in Illich, *Disabling Professions,* pp. 82-83.

4 National Council of Welfare, *In the Best Interests of the Child* (Ottawa: National Department of Health and Welfare, 1979), pp. 9-10.

5 Bernard, Lucas-White, and Moore, "Two Hands tied," p. 23.

6 Dale and Foster, *Feminists and State Welfare,* p. 99.

7 Helen Levine, "The Power Politics of Motherhood," in Turner and Emery, *Perspectives on Women,* p. 34.

8 Dale and Foster, *Feminists and State Welfare,* p. 99.

9 Shulman, *The Skills,* p. 56.

10 Daphne Statham, *Radicals in Social Work* (London: Routledge & Kegan Paul, 1978), p. 9.

11 William Schwartz, "On the Use of Groups in Social Work Practice," in William Schwartz and Serapio Zalba (eds.), *The Practice of Group Work* (New York: Columbia University, 1971), p. 11.

12 Shulman, *The Skills,* p. 67.

13 Dale and Foster, *Feminists and State Welfare,* p. 104.

14 Shulman, *The Skills,* p. 57.

15 Peter Silverman, *Who Speaks for the Children? The Plight of the Battered Child* (Toronto: General Publishing, 1978), p. 170.

Chapter 5: Managing Social Work: From Top to Bottom

1 Latimer, "An Analysis," p. 15.

2 Germain and Gitterman, *The Life Model,* p. 141.

3 Special Report of the Ombudsman, *An Investigation by the Alberta Ombudsman into the Foster Care Program,* Department of Social Services and Community Health, Alberta, March 1981, p. 22.

4 Joan Cummings, "Sexism in Social Work: The Experience of Atlantic
   Social Work Women," in *Atlantis,* Vol. 6, No. 3, Spring 1981, pp. 62-79.
5 Ibid., p. 68.
6 British Columbia Association of Social Workers, *Counterpoint: Women's
   Perspectives on Social Work,* B.C. Association of Social Workers'
   President's Task Force to Survey Sexism in Social Work, Vancouver,
   undated, p. 7.
7 Bonnie Jeffery and Martha Wiebe, "Women, Work and Welfare: The
   Saskatchewan Perspective," in *The Social Worker,* Vol. 50, No. 3, Fall
   1982, p. 118.
8 Nadya Tarasoff, "SW salaries in 1986: Would you rather boss a road
   gang?", *Ontario Association of Professional Social Workers,* Vol. 13, No.
   3, January 1987, p. 8.
9 Bernard, Lucas-White, and Moore, "Two Hands tied," p. 23.
10 See, for instance: Canada, House of Commons, *Indian Self-Government,*
   pp. 14-15; Patrick Johnston, *Native Children and the Child Welfare
   System* (Ottawa: Canadian Council on Social Development / James
   Lorimer, 1983); Canada, Dept. of Indian and Northern Affairs, *Indian
   Conditions: A Survey* (Ottawa, 1980). For an analysis of Native people,
   blacks, and Acadians in Nova Scotia, see Dorothy Moore,
   Multiculturalism: Myth or Reality?, Occasional paper no. 5, Halifax,
   Saint Mary's University International Education Centre, 1981.
11 Brad McKenzie, "Social Work Practice with Native People," in Shankar
   Yelaja (ed.), *An Introduction to Social Work Practice in Canada*
   (Toronto: Prentice-Hall, 1985), p. 274.
12 Ibid., p. 275.
13 This situation and the resulting occupation of the Indian Affairs office in
   Calgary were documented by anthropologist Joan Ryan in *Wall of Words:
   The Betrayal of the Urban Indian* (Toronto: Peter Martin, 1978).
14 Peter C. McMahon, *Management by Objectives in the Social Services*
   (Ottawa: Canadian Association of Social Workers, 1981).
15 Brian Segal and John Jackson, *Social Services Task Bank* (Ottawa: Centre
   for Social Welfare Studies, 1975).
16 Neil Tudiver, "Ideology and Management in the Social Services," paper
   presented to the Conference of the Canadian Association of Schools of
   Social Work, Saskatoon, June 1979, pp. 17, 28-29.
17 McMahon, *Management by Objectives,* p. 36.
18 Frédéric Lesemann, *Services and Circuses: Community and the Welfare
   State* (Montreal: Black Rose, 1984).

19 Juergen Werner Dankwort, "Regulating Social Workers: The Subordination of the Profession to its Industrial Relations System," Masters research report, School of Social Work, McGill University, Montreal, 1984.

20 Ernie S. Lightman, "The Impact of Government Economic Restraint on Mental Health Services in Canada," *Canada's Mental Health*, Vol. 34, No. 1, March 1986, p. 26. For a specific example, see *The Globe and Mail*, Nov. 1, 1986, p. 1, "Nursing Home Complaints Will Be Reviewed: Industry Confirms Aged are Beaten."

Chapter 6:
Unemployment to Welfare to Poverty: Clients Speak Out

1 See, for instance, *Social Infopac*, published by the Social Planning Council of Metropolitan Toronto, Vol. 5, No. 5, December 1986, for figures on unemployment and hidden unemployment in Canada.

2 Dorothy O'Connell, "Poverty: The Feminine Complaint," in Turner and Emery (eds.), *Perspectives on Women*, p. 47.

3 Eichler, "The Connection," p. 62.

4 *The Globe and Mail*, February 11, 1986.

5 Social Planning Council of Metro Toronto, *Report*, July 1986.

6 Study Team Report of the Task Force on Program Review, *Canada Assistance Plan*, Vol. 10 (Ottawa: Ministry of Supply and Services, 1986), p. 15. In addition the Metro Toronto Social Planning Council noted that: (a) From September 1981 to March 1983 the number of unemployed in Ontario doubled from 286,000 to 569,000. During that same period employable welfare cases nearly tripled, from slightly more than 27,000 to nearly 80,000 cases; and (b) there has been a substantial growth in the social assistance caseload since 1981 and this pattern has continued despite reduced levels of unemployment since 1983. See Social Planning Council of Metropolitan Toronto, *Living on the Margin: Welfare Reform for the Next Decade*, October 1986, pp. 20, 28.

7 *The Globe and Mail*, February 26, 1986.

8 Ibid.

9 See, for example, Statistics Canada, *The Labour Force* (Ottawa, September 1986), p. 74, which shows that about half of the unemployed had been without a job for seven months or more (without even counting

those who had given up looking for work); three-quarters of the unemployed had been without a job for over four months.

10 Harvey Brenner, *Estimating the Social Costs of National Economic Policy: Implications for Mental and Physical Health and General Aggression,* Joint Economic Committee of the Congress of the United States, October 1976; see also Leon Muszynski, "The Social Effects of Unemployment," in D. Paul Lumsden (ed.), *Community Mental Health Action: Primary Prevention Programming in Canada* (Ottawa: Canadian Public Health Association, 1984), p. 211.

11 Sharon Kirsh (ed.), *Unemployment: Its Impact on Body and Soul* (Toronto: Canadian Mental Health Association, 1983), p. 48.

12 Gordon Ternowetsky, "Federal Spending on the Private Sector, Profits and the Creation of Unemployment: Another Side of the Unemployment Insurance Review," in *SPAN: Canadian Review of Social Policy,* No. 14-15, May 1986, pp. 49-50.

13 Ibid., p. 52.

14 André Gorz, *Paths to Paradise: On the Liberation from Work* (London: Pluto, 1985), p. 71. For the importance of redefined work and of creating universal wage policies supplemented by income protection, see: Marvyn Novick, "Work and Well-Being: Social Choices for a Healthy Society," paper presented at the Public Interest Symposium on a New Work Agenda for Canada (Ottawa: Canadian Mental Health Association, October 1986). See also: Center for Popular Economics, *Economic Report of the People: An Alternative to the Economic Report of the President* (Boston: South End Press, 1986).

15 Graham Riches, *Food Banks and the Welfare Crisis,* (Ottawa: Canadian Council on Social Development, 1986), pp. 15, 147.

16 Lightman, "The Impact of Government Economic Restraint," p. 27.

17 A.B. Anderson, "Racism and Unemployment in the 'Outer City' of Metro Toronto," paper presented to the CSAA meeting, University of Guelph, June 1984, p. 18.

18 O'Connell, "Poverty," p. 47.

19 Levine, "The Personal Is Political," in Miles and Finn, *Feminism in Canada,* p. 191.

20 See Eli Zaretsky, "Rethinking the Welfare State: Independence, Economic Individualism and Family," in Dickinson and Russell (eds.), *Family, Economy and the State,* p. 93.

21 Levine, "The Personal Is Political," p. 192.

22 See Patricia Evans, "Work and Welfare: A Profile of Low-Income Single Mothers," *Canadian Social Work Review '84,* pp. 81-96.

23 Report of the Special Senate Committee on Poverty, *Poverty in Canada* (Ottawa: Information Canada, 1971), p. 83.

24 Louise Johnson, *Social Work Practice: A Generalist Approach* (Boston: Allyn and Bacon, 1983), p. 283.

25 Solicitor General Canada, *Annual Report 1979-1980* (Ottawa: Ministry of Supply and Services, 1981), p. 60.

26 Phyllis Chesler, *Women and Madness* (New York: Avon, 1972), p. 165; see also Leah Cohen, *Small Expectations: Society's Betrayal of Older Women* (Toronto: McClelland and Stewart, 1984), pp. 101-105, on nursing homes as abusive institutions.

27 Levine, "The Personal Is Political," p. 183.

28 Ibid., pp. 187-88.

29 Johnson, *Social Work Practice*, p. 284.

30 Social Planning Council of Metropolitan Toronto, *Living on the Margin*, p. 2.

31 "Preamble," *Canada Assistance Plan, 1966-67*, c. 45, s. 1.

32 *News Release,* Ministry of Human Resources, Victoria, B.C., August 27, 1981, announcing the new section 2(21) Regulations under the Guaranteed Available Income for Need Act.

33 In September 1986 the Ontario government agreed to abolish "man-in-the-house" regulations for single mothers who need welfare. *The Globe and Mail* reported this to be "a move that could inspire similar changes in other provinces". (*The Globe and Mail*, Sept. 19, 1986.)

34 Reuben Hasson, "The Cruel War: Social Security Abuse in Canada," *Canadian Taxation: A Journal of Tax Policy*, Vol. 3, No. 3, Fall 1981, p. 129.

35 Levine, "The Personal Is Political," p. 196.

36 Alberta Social Services and Community Health, *Child Welfare Programs*, 1 B.9, 1 C2(c). Emphasis added.

37 National Council of Welfare, *In the Best Interests of the Child*, pp. 17-18.

38 Canada, House of Commons, *Indian Self-Government in Canada* (Ottawa, 1983), p. 31; cited in *Taking Control Newsletter: A Review of Indian and Native Social Work Education in Canada*, Faculty of Social Work, University of Regina, No. 2, 1985, p. 4.

39 McKenzie, "Social Work Practice," p. 277.

40 Quoted in *Taking Control Newsletter*, p. 10.

41 Quoted in Jim Allison and Janice Johnson (eds.), *Say Hi to Julie: A Commentary from Children in Care in Alberta* (Calgary: Who Cares?, 1981), p. 49.

42 Ibid.

43 John Hylton, "Locking Up Indians in Saskatchewan: Some Recent Findings," in *Canadian Ethnic Studies,* Vol. XIII, No. 3, 1981, pp. 145-146.
44 Edmonton-Hobbema Review Committee, *Report* (Alberta: Indian Affairs, January 1977), p. 6.
45 Ibid., pp. 12-13.
46 Ibid., p. 12.
47 Quoted in Harvey Stalwick (ed.), *What Was Said? Study Guide One* (Regina: Faculty of Social Work, 1986), p. 11.
48 Ibid., p. 84.
49 Ibid., p. 11.
50 Quoted in Joan Ryan, *Wall of Words,* p. 84.

Chapter 7: Social Work and Social Change: Fighting Back

1 For critical alternatives to current employment and income floor programs, see Women's Research Centre, *Women and the Economy Kit* (Vancouver, 1986); Eichler, *Families in Canada Today*; Novich, "Work and Well-Being"; and Richard Powless, "Native People and Employment: A National Tragedy," in *Research Studies of the Commission on Equality in Employment* (Ottawa: Ministry of Supply and Services, 1985), pp. 606-608.
2 Jeffry Galper, *Social Work Practice: A Radical Perspective* (Englewood Cliffs, N.J.: Prentice-Hall, 1980), pp. 115-116.
3 John Gary Cameron, in John Gary Cameron and Patrick Kerans, "Social and Political Action," in Yelaja (ed.), *An Introduction to Social Work Practice,* p. 131.
4 Charlotte Bunch, "The Reformist Tool Kit," in *Quest Magazine,* Vol. 1, No. 1, 1974, p. 48.
5 Howard Buchbinder, "The Just Society Movement," in Brian Wharf (ed.), *Community Work in Canada* (Toronto: McClelland and Stewart, 1979), p. 131.
6 Cameron, "Social and Political Action," p. 117.
7 Buchbinder, "The Just Society Movement," pp. 141-151. See also Bill Lee, *Pragmatics of Community Organization* (Mississauga, Ont.: Common Act Press, 1986).

8 London Edinburgh Weekend Return Group, *In and Against the State* (London: Pluto, 1979), p. 83.

9 Gloria Norgang and Roger Roome (eds.), *For You, For Us: An Exploration of Lesbian and Gay Issues for the Helping Professional* (Ottawa: Pink Triangle Services, 1986).

10 Levine, "The Personal Is Political," p. 199.

11 McKenzie, "Social Work Practice with Native People," p. 285.

12 Angela Miles, "Ideological Hegemony in Political Discourse: Women's Specificity and Equality," in Miles and Finn (eds.), *Feminism in Canada*, p. 220.

13 Jillian Ridlington, "Providing Services the Feminist Way," in Maureen Fitzgerald, Connie Guberman, and Margie Wolfe (eds.), *Still Ain't Satisfied: Canadian Feminism Today* (Toronto: Women's Press, 1982), p. 96.

14 Cindy Player, "Government Funding of Battered Women's Shelter, Feminist Victory or Co-optation?" in *Breaking the Silence: A newsletter on feminism in social welfare research, action, policy and practice*, Vol. 1, No. 5, 1983, p. 4.

15 John Melichercik, "The Scope of Collective Bargaining in Social Welfare Organizations," in *The Social Worker*, Vol. 46, No. 1-2, Spring-Summer 1978, p. 32.

16 Galper, *Social Work Practice*, p. 163.

17 Ibid.

18 Denise Kouri, "Getting Organized in Saskatchewan," in Fitzgerald, Guberman and Wolfe (eds.), *Still Ain't Satisfied*, p. 167.

19 From a discussion, "What Are Our Options?" in Fitzgerald, Guberman and Wolfe (eds.), *Still Ain't Satisfied*, p. 306.

20 See, for example, *The Toronto Star*, Jan. 10, 1987, p. B11, and Jan. 14, 1987, p. A16.

21 Workers for Social Responsibility, *Insider Report*, No. 1 (Toronto: Ontario Public Service Employees' Union, 1984), p. 2.

22 Ibid., p. 5.

23 John Melichercik, "Collective Bargaining Through the Eyes of the Beholder," in *The Social Worker*, Vol. 45, No. 1, Spring 1977.

24 More specifically, at the executive (or director) level, in the eight agencies surveyed, there was no change in the attitude after unionization: two executives were positive, three were negative, and three were neutral. Among front-line social workers, prior to unionization 40 per cent were positive, another 40 per cent were neutral, and another 20 per cent were

negative; and after unionization 65 per cent were positive, 25 per cent were neutral and 10 per cent were negative. Melichercik, "Collective Bargaining," pp. 8-11. See also Ernie Lightman, "Social Workers, Strikes and Services to Clients," *Social Work*, Vol. 28, No. 2, March-April 1983.

25 From "What Are Our Options?" in Fitzgerald, Guberman and Wolfe (eds.), *Still Ain't Satisfied*, p. 301.

26 Eric Shragge, "Foreword" in Lesemann, *Services and Circuses*, pp. 20-21.

27 From "What Are Our Options?" in Fitzgerald, Guberman and Wolfe (eds.), *Still Ain't Satisfied*, p. 306.